CW01208511

Being
WARREN BUFFETT
LIFE LESSONS FROM A CHEERFUL BILLIONAIRE

Being WARREN BUFFETT

LIFE LESSONS FROM A CHEERFUL BILLIONAIRE

NIC LIBERMAN

Illustrations by Craig McGill

hardie grant books
MELBOURNE · LONDON

With gratitude to my Zaida Yankel and my dad, Bori;
and with hope and love to my boys,
Isaiah, Elon, Noah and Esha.

CONTENTS

INTRODUCTION VII
CHAPTER ONE LOVE 1
CHAPTER TWO LOYALTY 11
CHAPTER THREE INDEPENDENT THINKING 16
CHAPTER FOUR CONFIDENCE 22
CHAPTER FIVE OPTIMISM 25
CHAPTER SIX MODESTY AND HUMILITY 29
CHAPTER SEVEN CUTTING YOUR COAT 34
CHAPTER EIGHT PATIENCE 41
CHAPTER NINE DEFERRING GRATIFICATION 48
CHAPTER TEN FRUGALITY 55
CHAPTER ELEVEN CONSCIENCE 59
CHAPTER TWELVE GREED 64
CHAPTER THIRTEEN ENVY 70
CHAPTER FOURTEEN NARCISSISM 75
CONCLUSION 84

APPENDIX 89
NOTES 92
ACKNOWLEDGEMENTS 97

Introduction

HAVE YOU EVER wondered what it is about Warren Buffett that sets him apart? We know so much about the man and his work, yet the essence of his extraordinary success seems to have remained a mystery. What lies at the root of Buffett's remarkable achievements? Is it his involvement in the insurance business; his savvy with numbers; or because he is a 'value investor'? Perhaps it's just that he has been investing since he was a kid? Or, is he just lucky? However you look at it, none of these reasons alone reveals the essence of his genius. These factors are helpful pointers, but they are not the whole story. There is something that runs deeper, something more fundamental that underlies his mastery.

As a fairly young investor trying to understand and make sense of the countless investment styles and philosophies out there, something about Buffett and his charming and modest letters felt like home to me. Here was a man who seemed to provide the most obvious, simple and wise advice about some of the most complicated questions that plague any person thinking about investing. Coupled with that, he was enormously successful, humble and reachable. I was spellbound.

Yet, when turning to others in the hope of gleaning some insight into how it was that Buffett could actually do what he did, there seemed to be a dearth of understanding of the structure of the man that made it all possible. Sure, ideas abounded on the kinds of skills necessary to value a company, what kind of company he looked to invest in, or on some of his life experience, but nothing seemed to grapple with the question of what enabled this investment genius to accumulate wealth in the manner that he had. What set him apart? What was the foundation of this success?

Unlike Coca-Cola, Buffett has no heavily guarded secret recipe. He tells other investors exactly what he does and how they could do it. Yet, no one has come even close to matching his success.

Historically, very few investors have become extremely wealthy – as investors, not as businessmen. Until now, extraordinary wealth has primarily been amassed through highly specialised life-long involvements in particular businesses or industries – think of Rockefeller, Carnegie and Gates. But Buffett is different; he is an investor only in other people's businesses.

So, what does he have that no one else has ever had? What is so different or special about this man?

Nowhere I looked could I find any real answers.

I was completely intrigued and I needed to understand it. So I set out to interrogate every word this man ever wrote, asking of every sentence: Is this revelatory of his genius as an investor?

Clearly here was a man with a vast intellect and not only the wish to succeed but also the drive and resilience to devote a lifetime to the pursuit. This didn't answer the question, though, because there are plenty of people in the world with far superior intellects and much greater drives to succeed.

What I began to see was that Buffett was obviously a lot more than merely an intellectual giant with an unusual investment style. But I still did not know what it was that made him so special and unusual.

What I came to understand is that Buffett has a magical combination of particular personality qualities that facilitate greatness. His good fortune shouldn't daunt us however; there are things to be learned from it.

It is not only the particular features of his personality but the uniquely choreographed way they come together and relate to each other to produce the perfect essence of what is needed to invest in the way he does. What's most annoying is that this perfectly choreographed personality isn't choreographed at all.

Personality traits are embedded ways of being that are so formed and set that they seem natural to the individual in whom they reside. They are like deep furrows worn by water down a mountainside where the water habitually and naturally flows. If one tries to change the furrows by digging another channel, it doesn't take much of a storm before the water is running back down its habitual path. Much the same thing happens with the personality, which is the combination of character traits that provide the infrastructure for the way in which one deals with life. It's not what you are as a result of any particular effort, it's just who you naturally are. The rain simply has to fall and it will find its usual path. This does not suggest that it is impossible to change; nor does it limit people to the exact personalities they naturally form. It's merely saying that we all end up with a particular personality that is our default position. And boy did Buffett get lucky!

What follows is a description of the different dimensions of his personality that come together in interesting and unique ways to create the perfect storm.

And what evolved on the path to this answer was a wonderful journey of self-enquiry. Buffett became the vehicle for my own self-understanding; and I hope very much that some of my insights will travel with you on your own journey of exploration.

If, however, you picked up this book in the hope of finding a quick recipe for success, you will be disappointed. The aim of this book is to explore how we can be ourselves and still benefit from an understanding of the essential features that make up Buffett's genius as an investor.

CHAPTER ONE

Love

'FOR THE RIGHT BUSINESS – AND THE RIGHT PEOPLE – WE CAN PROVIDE A GOOD HOME.' WB

IT MIGHT SEEM a bit odd beginning a book about Warren Buffett and investing with a chapter on love. Making billions of dollars seems a bit more cold and remote than anything that could be explained by an understanding of love. But, for Buffett, everything begins with his relationship with money. It does not end there, however. Buffett's love of money and the way it spills over into the love of those who make it for him are important and unique because they have an impact that significantly contributes to his capacity to accumulate wealth in the way he does.

Buffett's consuming, life-long engagement with money seems more likely to be about love than anything else. The acquisition of money has single-mindedly held his interest for all of his life, no matter how

CHAPTER ONE

much money he has acquired. It's the only reason he gets involved in businesses. Indeed, much of his waking life is spent in the pursuit of acquiring it. It seems to mesmerise him. He explicitly states that making money holds no prestige or excitement for him. If you compare him with anyone who has an intense life-long interest in something, such as a stamp collector or a wine collector, you will find that they love their collections in similar ways. Buffett doesn't accumulate money for its instrumental value; or for what he could do with it. He seems much less interested in spending it than collecting it. He pursues it just to have more of it.

So what does this all mean and how can we understand this dynamic as a core feature of his investment success? What is love and why is it relevant to investing or, more specifically, to Buffett the investor?

The Beatles suggested: 'All you need is love'. Perhaps they were not wrong... or right. Love is integral to all the activities and engagements that give our lives their meaning. The intense level of emotional investment we make in certain people and activities is what stops life from becoming empty and pointless. If this book is concerned with the structure or essence of a man's brilliance as an investor, then love, which is the most fundamental of all investments – engagements with life – should be of central interest.

However, it is hard to reconcile such a life-giving emotional investment with all the froth and bubble that describes the everyday conception of love, which says: love is steadfast, love is kind, love is eternal, love has no envy, love is unconditional, love is uncompromising or love is everything. (Even Buffett himself has said that 'the most powerful force in the world is unconditional love'.)

The nature of Buffett's love of money and its relevance to his exceptional talent is important and significantly more sober than is commonly understood by many, including Buffett himself. The Beatles got it wrong in the sense of our over-idealised everyday conception of love, but seem to have got it right if one comes to understand more deeply the structure of love and the way it adheres us to life.

But, what is love?

In his book, *Love: A History*,[1] Simon May describes the fundamental structure that underlies all of our various experiences of love. He suggests that the basis of all love is 'a promise of or experience of someone or something that gives us a sense of at-homeness, rootedness or groundedness – something that touches us deeply in the right kind of combinations of ways'.[2] Love is the thing that provides an anchoring for our lives, makes us feel at home in our world, that we feel we have a place and are not alone.

May points out that our at-homeness begins with our mother and father and gradually branches out to encompass our work, our friends, our children, nature and all the things that really touch us in the right sort of way – even such things as money and status.

The appeal of May's notion of love is that it seems so real and true of our experience in all its complexity and ordinariness. It doesn't trap us with the demands and pressures of our modern handed-down understanding of love. It doesn't expect love to be eternal, unconditional, fully accepting, selfless, benevolent, harmonious; or to transport us to meaning, away from suffering. Love is not just about finding something pretty and lovable; it's about something in you being receptive to the right collection of qualities that make you feel at home with them.

Understood in this way, however, and only after the initial promise of groundedness and at-homeness has been fulfilled, does love begin to share some of the qualities commonly associated with romantic love, where there is a strong wish to possess, nurture and give everything to the object of our love.

CHAPTER ONE

So, if love is what gives us a sense of at-homeness, and deepens our sensation of being, then there is probably little doubt that Buffett loves money, and the people who make it for him. Once established, Buffett's love brings with it a strong wish to care for and give to those whom he loves. Because of their intimate association with his love of money, the managers and owners with whom Buffett works closely, become loved objects themselves.

Buffett's love of these managers and owners is a mature kind of love, which embraces and respects their separateness and different needs, despite the frustrations inherent in this. We could contrast this 'mature love' with a more primitive form where there is no recognition of the separateness of the other, who would be seen merely as an appendage that should immediately meet every one of our needs. Buffett's way of loving, which comes so naturally to him, creates an atmosphere in which the lover is encouraged to love, where his appreciation, recognition and support of the other makes them have loving feelings toward him.

As an investor and as someone whose investment style involves significant engagement with managers and owners, this capacity and way of being cannot be underestimated. He does not expect everything from the people he loves. The level of his maturity is further reflected in his capacity to deal with difficult tensions, impediments, disappointments and frustrations and still be able to love. This is not just the simpler, smoother, more romantic version of love that is more likely to be fragile and less enduring.

Buffett is never consumed by this love. He somehow manages to remain detached in his attachment. One could imagine that the managers who are devoted to him would feel highly worthwhile and valued, while at the same time feeling free and independent to do their own thing. Buffett explains:

LOVE

> 'Charlie Munger, our Vice Chairman, and I really have only two jobs. One is to attract and keep outstanding managers to run our various operations. Our main contribution has been to not get in their way. This approach seems elementary: if my job were to manage a golf team – and if Jack Nicklaus or Arnold Palmer were willing to play for me – neither would get a lot of directives from me about how to swing.[3]

> [M]y message to them [his managers] is simple: Run your business as if it were the only asset your family will own over the next hundred years. Almost invariably they do just that and, after taking care of the needs of their business, send excess cash to Omaha for me to deploy.'[4]

The depth of respect that Buffett shows to his managers facilitates one of the most compelling characteristics of love: the promise of at-homeness. Buffett's attitude towards those with whom he does business hits the spot. He tellingly says: 'For the right business – and the right people – we can provide a good home.'[5] These are not the words of a puppeteer pulling the strings of people in a contrived, planned way to make them feel at home. It would appear that Buffett has a natural way – something embedded in his nature – that makes the right people feel as valued as they do.

We know that the demands of ordinary life make it very hard for us to constantly let those close to us know how fully appreciated they are. Yet Buffett seems to do this with relative ease, despite having more than seventy of these relationships. It may be that he finds it easy to shower his managers and owners with what appears to be unconditional love because they consistently deliver on the promise of making more money.

One of Buffett's great gifts is the ability to select the right people to work with and then to create a respectful place for them to be free to devote themselves to the task at hand without interference from him. He says, 'My job is to make sure that I don't do anything that kills [my managers'] love of the business.'[6]

Explaining how he assesses people with whom he decides to go into business, he says: 'I look into their eyes and try to figure out whether they love the money, or if they love the business... If they don't love the business, I can't put [money] into it...'[7]

For Buffett, choosing the right people is crucial:

> 'Our attitude, however, fits our personalities and the way we want to live our lives. Churchill once said, "You shape your houses and then they shape you." We know the manner in which we wish to be shaped. For that reason, we would rather achieve a return of X while associating with people whom we strongly like and admire than realise 110 per cent of X by exchanging these relationships for uninteresting or unpleasant ones.'[8]

Choosing the right people also enables Buffett to satisfy his belief in long-term commitments. He makes choices at a deeper level and is committed to maintaining them over time, but he also expects owners to take responsibility for making themselves rich by nurturing that part of their enterprise that they continue to own. 'We need 80 per cent... It is important to us that the family members who run the business remain as owners,' he says.[9]

This kind of relationship is not characterised by manipulation and rapacious control. Instead it is one that creates a co-operative, mutual connection through which people feel cared for and experience themselves as separate, valued individuals. It allows his business associates to love him in return and to work for him with gratitude, joy and willingness, combining their own self-interest with his. Buffett explains: 'People... find working for Berkshire Hathaway to be almost identical to running their own show.'[10]

Perhaps one of the greatest impediments to being able to love another is envy. Envy destroys love and gratitude. If we look at the essence of what we all recognise and are amused by in Gore Vidal's quote, 'When a friend of mine succeeds, a little something in me dies', we realise that our amusement comes from the way in which Vidal reveals our wish to destroy or diminish the object of our envy. But, if our friend's superior success is what we wish to draw on to make us rich, we would find ourselves in trouble. The inability to be grateful for their capacity would spoil our ready access to what they have to offer.

Buffett's capacity to find contentment and a self-affirming sense of his value within, rather than in relation to, others is central to his ability to seek out gifted individuals and celebrate their superior strength while harnessing it for his own wealth creation. Being at peace with envy is a crucial element of both the way in which Buffett can be grateful to the people who make him rich, and they can be grateful to him. This is a big part of how they can love each other.

The particular intensity of Buffett's relationship with money and the people who make it for him has created the kind of workplace environment that every owner dreams of: people who are devoted to creating wealth for him while feeling completely at home and integrated with the enterprise of making money for him and themselves. He is explicit about this when he says: 'It is a real pleasure to work with managers who enjoy coming to work each morning and, once there, instinctively and unerringly think like owners. We are associated with some of the very best.'[11]

It is neither money nor capital that he gives them that makes them devoted to him, it is the way he loves them. One cannot understate this dynamic as one of the fundamental ingredients of Buffett's incredible

CHAPTER ONE

success as an investor.

Evidently, Buffett chooses his people conditionally. He says:

> 'When you have able managers of high character running businesses about which they are passionate, you can have a dozen or more reporting to you and still have time for an afternoon nap. Conversely, if you have one person reporting to you who is deceitful, inept or uninterested, you will find yourself with more than you can handle. Charlie and I could work with twice the number of managers we now have, so long as they had the rare qualities of the present ones... For good reason, we had very high expectations when we joined with these managers. In every case, however, our experience has greatly exceeded those expectations. We have received far more than we deserve, but we are willing to accept such inequities. (We subscribe to the view Jack Benny expressed upon receiving an acting award: "I don't deserve this but, then, I have arthritis and I don't deserve that either.")'[12]

Our modern view of love as being selfless and unconditional – where the object of our love is loved for itself and not for ourselves – leaves us wondering how we can make sense of Buffett's love. He clearly puts a lot of effort into choosing people to love who are specifically going to be making him a lot of money. Only such people get through the eye of the needle into his heart. To make it more confusing, he seems to love them with all the genuine elements of commitment, loyalty, affection, respect – for themselves and their inherent value – without necessarily wanting to use or control them in specific ways. It's a puzzle. If he is simply 'using' them to make money, is he really loving them? Or, more specifically, is he really loving them because he is 'using' them? The answer to the latter is probably yes, and it is the writings of May that make some sense of this. May has no illusions about love being selfless. Indeed for May there is no conflict of principle between self-interest and love. He describes love in a way that perfectly fits with our understanding of Buffett. He suggests that initially love is quite selfish in that it occurs when we find someone or something that meets our own needs for rootedness, belonging, at-homeness, or making us feel alright in the world. And goes on to say that once that need has been met, all the other traditionally understood qualities of love – the altruism of love, the giving over, the will to die for another, the wish to pursue and possess – seem to flow quite generously.

What is completely fundamental to Buffett, the genius investor, and Buffett, one of the wealthiest men in the world, is his love of money. It's the love of money that gives him his sense of place, of groundedness, and at-homeness in the world. The material money in the world is almost hypothetical for him. It's the love of it that drives and sustains him. It is the very nature of money itself that makes him love it. It's not artwork, it's not sex, it's not fine wine or Ferraris. It's money that touches him deeply in the right combination of ways. More than anything, money does it for him.

The unique place of money in his mind is revealed in his humorous but revealingly unorthodox lack of appreciation of the significance of the Voyages of Discovery. He almost dismisses their value in light of the opportunity cost involved in not compounding the initial investment in the exploration:

> 'I have it from unreliable sources that the cost of the voyage Queen Isabella originally underwrote for Columbus in 1492 was approximately $30,000. This has been considered at least a moderately successful utilisation of venture capital. Without attempting to evaluate the psychic income derived from

CHAPTER ONE

finding a new hemisphere, it must be pointed out that, even had squatter's rights prevailed, the whole deal was not exactly another IBM. Figured very roughly, the $30,000 invested at four per cent compounded annually would have amounted to something like $2,000,000,000,000 (that's $2 trillion for those of you who are not government statisticians) by 1962. Historical apologists for the Indians of Manhattan may find refuge in similar calculations. Such fanciful geometric progressions illustrate the value of either living a long time, or compounding your money at a decent rate. I have nothing particularly helpful to say on the former point.'[13]

What is clearer than any speculation about the origins of his love for money is that, somewhere along the way, making money became at-homeness for Buffett, and that is what makes him so rich. It's natural for him to want to make money. It's not forced; it's not about secondary gain. It's not as if some part of him knows the other part should get up and get going to make some money. All the elements are completely in tune. There is no jagged aspect; it's a perfect symphony. And that is why he skips to work and feels so blessed: because he is having a love affair; he is having a love affair every day with his cherished lover – money.

Loyalty

'IT'S HARD TO TEACH A NEW DOG OLD TRICKS.' WB

IN THE PREVIOUS chapter, I suggest that Buffett's love of making money leads him to commit to long-term relationships, among other things. He has very strong attachments to the people and things that matter in his life, which shows up as a 'loyal engagement' in his world. Loyalty permeates not only his relationships but also the way in which he does business.

What do I mean by loyalty? To me, loyalty is characterised by a certain sticking by or ongoing attachment, where the attachment is not dependent on whether or not it is useful or advantageous. Loyalty is something beyond a mutually beneficial transaction.

As with love, loyalty does not necessarily have selfless beginnings; nor is it something that we can develop toward just anybody. We can be loyal to particular people who meet our needs (which we may not

CHAPTER TWO

fully appreciate or understand) in particular ways and with whom we can form a specific kind of connection. But there is no doubt that a relationship that starts off based on usefulness or advantage, can progress to a much stickier place. Once you become loyal, you develop a more-than-rational attachment. I'm not saying that loyalty is irrational; but that its adhesive power goes beyond mere rationality. The presence of the rational also means, however, that it can be broken by certain levels of disadvantage, pain or loss. Loyalty is robust but by no means indestructible.

Loyalty has a transcendental quality that raises it above the ordinary conditions of friendship. It's not just love or affection or familiarity or trust or devotion – it's loyalty. Loyalty doesn't 'sort of' exist. One is either loyal or not loyal. It's really a bit like butter. When you whisk cream long enough, it suddenly turns into butter. It's not possible to have butter that is half butter and still half cream. After the cream has been beaten past a certain threshold it suddenly becomes butter. So it is with loyalty. There comes a point where one's attunement with a person transforms from association, affection and trust into loyalty... and from then on it's butter!

Some of Buffett's loyal attachments certainly seem to develop on a rational basis, where he is motivated originally by the wish to make money. He carefully and consciously selects the people he wishes to work with on the basis of their ability to make him money and his level of comfort with them.

Buffett's loyal attachments go beyond business managers and people who make him money. He becomes loyally attached to his houses, his office, his restaurants, the candy he eats, and much more. In some respects, this facet of his loyalty may well be a tool that allows him to enhance the safe, familiar world that he has created for himself. It also seems to free him up to focus his energies on his work without his resources being taken up by managing change and disruption: 'Management changes, like marital changes, are painful, time-consuming and chancy.' (This particular dimension of loyalty - his enchantment with stability and familiarity - is highly specific to Buffett and certainly wouldn't suit anyone who is stimulus hungry.)

Buffett did not necessarily receive a higher-than-usual dose of loyalty in his genetic make-up. It's not the amount of loyalty he applies that's different; it is the way in which he applies it in his dealings with the owners and managers of his businesses that gives him a particular edge as an investor.

The wellbeing of his loyally held companies is bound up with his own wellbeing. The level of identification that comes with the deep involvement means that the persons or companies to which he is loyal become *his - his businesses, his people.* Buffett's commitment to and affection for his people seem to develop a transcendental quality, rather than remaining solely linked to their capacity to make money for him. 'Regardless of price, we have no interest at all in selling any good business that Berkshire owns, and are very reluctant to sell sub-par businesses as long as we expect them to generate at least some cash and as long as we feel good about their managers and labour relations.'[1] (It can be seen in the case with the Berkshire Hathaway textile mill that, despite its ongoing unprofitability, his attachment to it created a reticence to make a strictly 'commercial' decision... for a while.)

Buffett is no less vulnerable than the rest of us to the unrealistically wonderful, life-affirming madness of the strong bonds of attachment and commitment that tie him to his people. He is both financially better off and much happier in his working life because he treats the people he works with as whole people, not as mere functions. He doesn't avoid the additional effort that comes with treating people in this particular way. He chooses people carefully and treats them as though they matter to him, because they do, and they realise they do.

The effects of Buffett's loyalty on people who work for him give them a strong sense of place, belonging, security, and a capacity to devote themselves to him by forming equally loyal attachments. This also has the positive outcome of encouraging owners who have formed life-long attachments to their businesses to feel safe to sell their businesses to Buffett. (See Appendix for a revealing example of how Buffett goes about making people feel safe.)

One cannot be blamed for wondering whether it is possible to be truly loyal to more than seventy businesses. But there can be no doubt that Buffett's particular style leads to his partners in business feeling loyally protected and looked after by him. It seems to be a much more complex attunement than mere numbers indicate. It's not about how many people he has in his fold; it's about the nature of the relationships he develops with each of them, perhaps more accurately revealed when he says: 'Agatha Christie, whose husband was an archaeologist, said that was the perfect profession for one's spouse: "The older you become, the more interested they are in you."'[2]

This reflects his ability to have a deepening appreciation of a maturing relationship over time with the same person. There is an increasing interest, attachment and involvement, rather than boredom or detachment. He emphasises this again: 'It's hard to teach a new dog old tricks.'[3]

Once he has picked the individuals he likes, trusts and admires, he enjoys their quirks. He backs his people, stays out of their way and lets them do their tricks. He loves his 'old dogs'.

He describes this beautifully:

> 'Our goal is to attract long-term owners who, at the time of purchase, have no timetable or price target for sale but plan instead to stay with us indefinitely. We don't understand the

CEO who wants lots of stock activity, for that can be achieved only if many of his owners are constantly exiting. At what other organisation - school, club, church, etc. - do leaders cheer when members leave? (However, if there was a broker whose livelihood depended upon the membership turnover in such organisations, you could be sure that there would be at least one proponent of activity, as in: "There hasn't been much going on in Christianity for a while; maybe we should switch to Buddhism next week.")'[4]

Perhaps what is reflected here runs much deeper than it would appear at first glance. He has very deep roots, a sense of security, a strong sense of himself and, most of all, a solid, stable foundation from which to take on the enormous challenges he does in a calm and unhurried way. He is, after all, a man who has lived in the same town, in the same street, eaten at the same restaurants, worked in the same building and stuck to the same couple of wives for most of his life! It may be that this 'constricted' life, characterised by long-term relationships, contributes significantly to his strength.

Despite Buffett's loyalty having its beginnings in his relationships with people who are devoted to making him rich, it is quite clear that he moves to a genuinely loyal commitment to them for the more-than-rational, strong emotional ties that loyalty brings with it. The impact of this kind of loyalty on his wealth creation is that it stirs, in turn, a ferocious loyalty in those who work for him and make money for him. The way he sticks by his people has a multiplier effect on his returns. This loyalty provides him with a stable of dedicated and devoted partners and managers who, once chosen for their gift at making money, can almost be left alone to continue growing his wealth.

CHAPTER THREE

Independent thinking

'A PUBLIC OPINION POLL IS NO SUBSTITUTE FOR THOUGHT.' WB

A LARGE PART of Buffett's success can be ascribed to his ability to think independently. He is his own man. He stands his ground and comes to his own conclusions; and he is relatively untouched by the multitude of views that surround him. This unique talent of his is something that very few of us manage to master.

The German philosopher Martin Heidegger[1] provides some insight into why we humans find it quite hard to think independently. He speaks of the notion of 'a falling into the they', when individuals lose themselves in relation to the views and expectations of others. He suggests that there is no such thing as a pure separate individual in the world; an isolated 'I' without others. We live in relation to others and are always in some way concerned with them. The pressure to compromise is unrelenting, which means that we live in a constant state of tension between being ourselves and losing ourselves.

Of course we are generally unaware of the extent to which we absorb the common view or the views of our significant others and, although we are largely oblivious of this process taking place, we give these received attitudes, values and opinions a certainty and authority. This pre-reflective absorption of what is around us leads us to adopt the conventional path, as reflected in comments like 'the property market will always go up' (until it doesn't!). The fact that this may or may not be true is irrelevant. The point is that this attitude is often absorbed without thinking, rather than after thinking. This is the kind of idle talk Heidegger refers to as having, to some extent, second-hand or closed-off meanings, and these meanings are embedded in language in such a way that they give the idle talk an authoritative character of certainty.

Finding a balance between being ourselves and taking on the opinions of others is no mean feat. How does one keep the influence of others at bay, cordoned off from a space in which one can have one's own thoughts?

Edmund Husserl,[2] the philosopher and founder of phenomenology, offers a clue. He suggests we search for the truth by 'bracketing' as many of our preconceptions as we can. This, he said, would help us to understand the world independently of both the way others see it and of our own prejudices. A practice such as this could be the beginning of thinking independently and openly, and would allow the world to reveal itself more clearly.

One can't help feeling the ability to think independently, as described above, comes naturally to Buffett. He is one of those rare individuals who is able to stem the tide of others' opinions so that he can allow his own thoughts to emerge. While a struggle for independence is a

CHAPTER THREE

significant dimension of ordinary life in a shared world where there is a constant pull to adapt, it rockets into a different league entirely when one attempts to do this in an investment environment.

Investing is an orientation towards a fantasised future in which the investor feels a responsibility to succeed and believes his success or otherwise will reflect directly on him. He is vulnerable because his decisions are going to determine the shape of his world, often with enormous financial consequences. No wonder then that it is very difficult not to feel influenced by the many strongly held views that prevail in an industry that is, by its very nature and by its reward mechanisms, a distillation of the views and opinions of thousands of disparate individuals.

This world of coalesced random opinions, which ultimately determine the price of an investment at any given point in time, is playfully referred to by Buffett's mentor, Benjamin Graham, as 'Mr Market'. In the following quote from Buffett[3] about Mr Market he describes to us his journey toward independent thinking:

> 'Ben Graham, my friend and teacher, long ago described the attitude toward market fluctuations that I believe to be most conducive to investment success. He said that you should imagine market quotations as coming from a remarkably accommodating fellow named Mr Market who is your partner in a private business. Without fail, Mr Market appears daily and names a price at which he will either buy your interest or sell you his.
>
> Even though the business that the two of you own may have economic characteristics that are stable, Mr Market's quotations will be anything but. For, sad to say, the poor fellow has incurable emotional problems. At times he feels euphoric and

can see only the favourable factors affecting the business. When in that mood, he names a very high buy-sell price because he fears that you will snap up his interest and rob him of imminent gains. At other times he is depressed and can see nothing but trouble ahead for both the business and the world. On these occasions he will name a very low price, since he is terrified that you will unload your interest on him.

Mr Market has another endearing characteristic: He doesn't mind being ignored. If his quotation is uninteresting to you today, he will be back with a new one tomorrow. Transactions are strictly at your option. Under these conditions, the more manic-depressive his behaviour, the better for you.

But, like Cinderella at the ball, you must heed one warning or everything will turn into pumpkins and mice: Mr Market is there to serve you, not to guide you. It is his pocketbook, not his wisdom, that you will find useful. If he shows up some day in a particularly foolish mood, you are free to either ignore him or to take advantage of him, but it will be disastrous if you fall under his influence. Indeed, if you aren't certain that you can understand and value your business far better than Mr Market, you don't belong in the game. As they say in poker, "If you've been in the game for thirty minutes and you don't know who the patsy is, you're the patsy."

Ben's Mr Market allegory may seem out-of-date in today's investment world, in which most professionals and academics talk of efficient markets, dynamic hedging and betas. Their interest in such matters is understandable, since techniques shrouded in mystery clearly have value to the purveyor of investment advice. After all, what witch doctor has ever achieved fame and fortune by simply advising "take two aspirins"? Rather an investor will succeed by coupling good business judgement with an ability to insulate his thoughts and behaviour from the super-contagious emotions that swirl about the marketplace. In my own efforts to stay insulated, I have found it highly useful to keep Ben's Mr Market concept firmly in mind.'

Buffett explains how he avoids getting lost in the common view by pointing to what he regards as true conservatism. He juxtaposes the conservation of capital with traditional conservatism, which is 'the done thing':

> 'It is unquestionably true that the investment companies have their money more conventionally invested than we do. To many people conventionality is indistinguishable from conservatism. In my view, this represents erroneous thinking. Neither a conventional nor an unconventional approach, per se, is conservative.
>
> Truly conservative actions arise from intelligent hypotheses, correct facts and sound reasoning. These qualities may lead to conventional acts, but there have been many times when they have led to unorthodoxy. In some corner of the world they are probably still holding meetings of the Flat Earth Society.
>
> We derive no comfort because important people, vocal people, or great numbers of people agree with us. Nor do we derive comfort if they don't. A public opinion poll is no substitute for thought. When we really sit back with a smile on our face is when we run into a situation we can understand, where the facts are ascertainable and clear, and the course of action obvious. In

that case – whether conventional or unconventional – whether others agree or disagree – we feel – we are progressing in a conservative manner.'[4]

Buffett sees nothing magical in his capacity to think independently. He has a lifetime of accumulated skill in assessing the value of businesses and invests only in businesses he can understand because it is when you do not fully understand something that your opinions can more easily be swayed. His general attitude toward 'opinion' is one of grave wariness. He is very clear that others' opinions are no substitute for a commitment to 'intelligent hypotheses, correct facts and sound reasoning', and he distances himself from what other people – 'important people, vocal people, or great numbers of people' – do or don't think. So, while thinking independently might not come as naturally to most as it does to Buffett, one could move in that direction by avoiding the inherent pull towards shared views of the world.

To be independent one has to be one's own person – oneself. I do not suggest that we should be so cut off and independently self-sufficient that we deny the importance of the relationships we depend on and draw from. I am pointing to an independence of knowing who one is and being faithful to oneself, despite the complexities of living in a shared world with all of its swirling influences.

To be an independent thinker, one cannot rely on significant amounts of knowledge and skill alone; in the end, it requires the strength of character that allows one to stand steady in the midst of strong currents of opinion. Buffett possesses the strength of character to be firm in these currents. This is helped in a small way by his strong sense of place in Omaha, 'far from the madding crowd'.

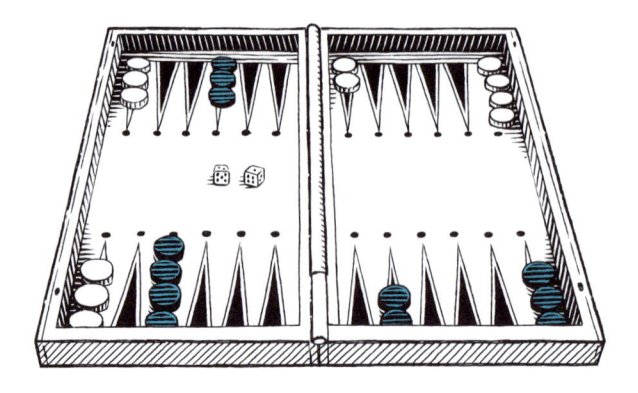

Confidence

'I'M NO GENIUS, I'M SMART IN SPOTS – BUT I STAY AROUND THOSE SPOTS.' WB

THE NATURE OF Buffett's confidence is very specific. It is a healthy confidence. It's a kind of confidence that occupies that helpful and creative space between the extremes of over-confidence and timid impotence.

Confidence is generally seen as having a sense of one's own worth, a feeling of boldness or assuredness, but there is another dimension to confidence, one that provides a certain degree of inner restraint. Real confidence is a grounded, realistic faith in one's capacity for mastery. It has a flavour of a contained, open, solid capability, a capability to act upon the world.

Confidence, in its broadest sense, seems to involve certain temperamental 'givens'. As they grow up, some children seem to have, as part of their genetic good luck or perhaps as a result of very early experiences, the ability to engage openly with the world. They seem to feel that they belong. They feel interesting, worthwhile and capable. Confidence may also develop in a context where individuals are in a respectful and affectionate relationship with someone in whose eyes they can see their own good reflected. They can draw on and take into themselves what the other sees.

It may well be that these two dimensions of confidence have been part of Buffett's development. However, what is most obvious when reading his writings, is the way in which a third element of confidence has grown in him. This element emerges from the freedom he has given himself to spend sufficient time to develop a sense of mastery in his areas of expertise. This is most strikingly revealed in Buffett's frequent citing of the Thomas Watson Snr (early president of IBM) quote: 'I'm no genius, I'm smart in spots – but I stay around those spots.'[1]

This implies an incredible modesty in what one expects of oneself. That everything need not be done well or at the highest level; limitations can be accepted without anguish or torment or being envious of others; and one can sit comfortably being good at only a few things. Having discerning and limited expectations of oneself allows a realistic confidence to develop.

The oft-repeated cliché that you can do anything if you are smart, doesn't easily fool him. He seems to accept that it is necessary to limit one's interests if you are to spend the time necessary to build up serious confidence. And 'interest' seems to be a relevant issue here. We know that, generally speaking, one of the elements necessary to build confidence in an area is real interest. Without it, particularly in an area in which one may feel weak, it becomes extremely difficult to stay engaged long enough to develop confidence.

Increasingly, it seems for investors in general and for Buffett in particular, that confidence is about not stretching oneself too far. It is a powerful thing if we can stay in our good spots long enough to build up confidence slowly. Buffett thrives in his spots and he has stayed in those spots for sufficient time to create the kind of familiarity and deeply intimate understanding that ignites confidence to the point where he can make sound, independent judgements. It also prevents him from drawing the fallacious conclusion that he is good at everything because he's good at a few things. He just gets on with the things he is good at and does them well.

Because Buffett is largely free of envy, he is happy to stay comfortably in his own good spots without being distracted by wanting to emulate the good spots of others. He has the capacity to say, 'I'm good at only this', however impressive or unimpressive it is. He gets on with getting to know it well, without constantly looking over his shoulder to see whether or not the more impressive people are doing more impressive things.

Perhaps Henry Hazlitt, a renowned economist and political writer, summed up this dynamic when he said: 'The highest pre-eminence in any one study commonly arises from the concentration of the attention and the faculties on that one study. He who expects from a great name in politics, in philosophy, in art, equal greatness in other things, is little versed in human nature.'[2]

Buffett seems to have developed a deep inner confidence, based on both the sense of his own value and the fruits of accumulated experience, by spending so much time with so few things.

CHAPTER FIVE

Optimism

'TO EARN EVEN 15 PER CENT ANNUALLY OVER THE NEXT DECADE… WE WOULD NEED PROFITS AGGREGATING ABOUT $3.9 BILLION. ACCOMPLISHING THIS WILL REQUIRE A FEW BIG IDEAS – SMALL ONES JUST WON'T DO. CHARLIE MUNGER, MY PARTNER IN GENERAL MANAGEMENT, AND I DO NOT HAVE ANY SUCH IDEAS AT PRESENT, BUT OUR EXPERIENCE HAS BEEN THAT THEY POP UP OCCASIONALLY. [HOW'S THAT FOR A STRATEGIC PLAN?]' WB

WARREN BUFFETT appeared on the cover of *Time* magazine, for the first time in 2012, under the heading 'The Optimist'.[1] In the cover article, by Rana Foroohar, Buffett insists 'his optimism isn't emotional but quantitative'. In other words, Buffett's particular brand of optimism is thought through, calculated and realistic. This is not the usual kind of optimism, which is most commonly understood as a tendency to expect the best possible outcome or dwell on the most hopeful aspects of a situation. This definition is far too overstated and unrestrained to be applied to Buffett.

Buffett's mostly positive view about the outcome of his investment activities is based on a much more cautious, restrained understanding of the things he is positive about. He doesn't easily slip into over-generalising the optimistic aspects of a particular situation: 'Both our operating and investment experience cause us to conclude that 'turnarounds' seldom turn, and that the same energies and talent are much better employed in a good business purchased at a fair price than in a poor business purchased at a bargain price.'[2]

In the ordinary sense, optimism can be seen as an attitude towards or faith in the future, which, despite dangers and possible hiccups, assumes that things will ultimately turn out in a positive way. This is not a position taken lightly by Buffett. He isn't just blithely optimistic. His optimism is based on the solid foundation of mastery. His own repeated experience has shown him that he can make the world work for him; and that opportunities will continue to present themselves. In this way he is freed from an agitated panic about future possibilities. This is a kind of optimism that is based on a long-term, steeped, restrained understanding of his activities; it makes it possible for him to sit through what are sometimes scary moments while retaining a hopeful outlook overall. Buffett reveals his optimism about the future in the way he is patiently able to be part of a flow of economic activities without having to over-control them. He says:

> 'To earn even 15 per cent annually over the next decade... we would need profits aggregating about $3.9 billion. Accomplishing this will require a few big ideas – small ones just won't do. Charlie Munger, my partner in general management, and I do not have

any such ideas at present, but our experience has been that they pop up occasionally. [How's that for a strategic plan?]'[3]

It's the experience of discovering opportunities over a lifetime's work that gives Buffett his optimism, not some insubstantial hope.

Buffett's optimism gains its health from the way it is closely intertwined with a realistic view of the investment world and its dangers. For example, he says:

> 'We expect our insurance business to both grow and make significant amounts of money – but progress will be distinctly irregular and there will be major unpleasant surprises from time to time. It's a treacherous business and a wary attitude is essential. We must heed Woody Allen: "While the lamb might sleep with the lion, the lamb shouldn't count on getting a whole lot of sleep."'[4]

So, while his optimism is contained by his realistic acceptance of perils, it is sufficiently strong to allow him to spend the night with the lion rather than avoid the dangers involved in enterprises that may be very profitable but hazardous. A more timid man who is more pessimistic might see only the dangers and avoid the insurance business altogether. He seems to have struck just the right balance between keeping his feet on the ground and being hopeful.

Again, this sober attitude toward an optimistic engagement with the investment enterprise combined with a solid respect for the fundamentals is revealed when Buffett says:

> 'At Berkshire, we have no view of the future that dictates what businesses or industries we will enter. Indeed, we think it's usually poison for a corporate giant's shareholders if it embarks upon new ventures pursuant to some grand vision. We prefer

instead to focus on the economic characteristics of businesses that we wish to own and the personal characteristics of managers with whom we wish to associate – and then hope we get lucky in finding the two in combination.'[5]

To sustain an optimistic attitude toward the future, it's not uncommon for business people to deny the dangers ahead and present only a favourable picture. Buffett seems to have no need to do this and he is quite easily able to hold onto his optimism with a clear understanding of the limitations of life:

'Our gain in net worth during the year was $613.6 million, or 48.2 per cent. It is fitting that the visit of Halley's Comet coincided with this percentage gain: neither will be seen again in my lifetime.'[6]

Poor Buffett, having to drop down from a 48 per cent return but, as he says when he quotes Sam Goldwyn: '"In life, one must learn to take the bitter with the sour."'[7]

Buffett's optimism gives him a solid, quiet capacity to endure the vicissitudes of some business decisions without becoming jumpy or impulse ridden. This capacity gives him a significant advantage over the rest of us mere mortals who may manage these tensions much less elegantly.

CHAPTER SIX

Modesty and humility

'WE WILL NOT NORMALLY PAY A LOT
IN ANY PURCHASE FOR WHAT WE ARE SUPPOSED
TO BRING TO THE PARTY – FOR WE FIND THAT
WE DON'T ORDINARILY BRING A LOT.' WB

WHAT COMES MOST strongly to mind when thinking of Buffett's legendary modesty and humility are the words of James G. March: 'In the end, you know, we are very minor blips in a cosmic story. Aspirations for importance or significance are the illusions of the ignorant. All our hopes are minor, except to us; but some things matter because we choose to make them matter. What might make a difference to us, I think, is whether in our tiny roles, in our brief time, we inhabit life gently and add more beauty than ugliness.'[1]

If modesty, as March suggests, is about an awareness of our smallness in the scheme of things, then Buffett is inherently modest. He is not only

CHAPTER SIX

very aware of his smallness in relation to the most successful money-making businessmen in the world, he can very easily recognise their larger stature and actively pursue them to be part of his larger stable. Buffett constantly acknowledges the limited and connected role that he plays in something so much bigger than himself. This world view is far away from the omnipotence and self-importance that characterise a good part of the investment environment today.

Buffett is able to calmly accept his limitations and his part in things greater than himself. In fact he revels in it; he makes most of his money by seeking out people who he knows are better than himself and is delighted that they are so. He then attaches himself to them and draws on their greater capacities to enrich himself. His awareness of his limits comes through when he says:

> '... after twenty-five years of buying and supervising a great variety of businesses, Charlie and I have not learned how to solve difficult business problems. What we have learned is to avoid them. To the extent we have been successful, it is because we concentrated on identifying one-foot hurdles that we could step over rather than because we acquired any ability to clear seven footers.'[2]

The humble can bear to be small because they don't live in relation to others or use comparison as a means of knowing themselves. Buffett isn't pushed by the fear of humiliation to puff himself up. He is comfortable about not being competent in or knowledgeable about everything. There is no desire to try to cover it up or make himself 'not small'. He has sufficient self-esteem to allow himself to be limited and have the luxury of modesty.

But is Buffett's relationship with modesty entirely genuine? One can't help feeling that it is false modesty when, year after year, he claims that it is unlikely he will do as well next year as he did last year. Any look at the history of his activities would suggest the opposite, perhaps even to him if he were honest in this regard.

Here is a familiar refrain:

> '... the results of the first ten years have absolutely no chance of being duplicated or even remotely approximated during the next decade. They may well be achieved by some hungry twenty-five-year old working with $105,100 initial partnership capital and operating during a ten-year business and market environment, which is frequently conducive to successful implementation of his investment philosophy. This will not be achieved by a better fed thirty-six-year old working with our $54,065,345 current partnership capital who presently finds perhaps one-fifth to one-tenth as many really good ideas as previously to implement his investment philosophy.'[3]

No doubt as one reads this, one can be easily enchanted by the seeming modesty, but perhaps only the first few dozen times. Then the question arises: Is this a trick that allows him to reduce his performance-anxiety, freeing himself to 'tap dance to work' and enjoy what he does without the weight of expectation? If one can imagine that Buffett does fall prey to pressures and expectations, such a construct could even be a core part of Buffett's mastery.

The evidence however suggests that he is realistic. 'Charlie ... never lets me forget Ben Franklin's advice: "A small leak can sink a great ship."'[4] He is aware of how important it is to think things through and he is also aware of how a certain kind of mistake can bring everything down. He's not complacent or omnipotent; nor is he paralysed or inhibited by the fear of making mistakes. He looks at life as it is.

These twin faculties of modesty and humility offer a perfect

CHAPTER SIX

counterbalance to omnipotence. The business world is littered with the tragic ends of talented people who have taken a hop, skip and a jump from a realistic outlook to a belief that they can do anything because they have achieved a measure of success. Omnipotence is a kind of manic denial of the vulnerabilities and dangers of the world. It blinkers one's ability to see things clearly and reduces the capacity of the mind to be open enough to make sound and clear judgements.

Omnipotence is the Icarus of optimism and confidence, where healthy optimism and confidence feed on themselves too much and judgement becomes distorted. Icarus, as described in Greek mythology, was the son of a cautious father, Daedalus, who made himself and his son wax and feather wings to fly out of their prison walls. Daedalus warned his son of the excitement of flying and to be wary of flying too high and too close to the sun. Upon taking flight, Icarus' excitement couldn't be contained and led to deadly omnipotence, as his wings melted nearing the sun.

Omnipotently distorting a perception of the world in this way is worlds away from Buffett's attitude:

> '... what we do know, however, is that occasional outbreaks of those two super-contagious diseases, fear and greed, will forever occur in the investment community. The timing of these epidemics will be unpredictable, and the market aberrations produced by them will be equally unpredictable, both as to duration and degree. Therefore, we never try to anticipate the arrival or departure of either disease. Our goal is more modest: we simply attempt to be fearful when others are greedy and to be greedy only when others are fearful.'[5]

Buffett is not an unrealistically optimistic man. He is aware that certain mistakes can be crippling; and he is aware that there are dangers and pitfalls even in the most positive times. But it is Buffett's modesty and restraint that help him to avoid making that one fatal error that omnipotence is always inviting. He makes his judgements in the solid reality of things that he can understand from the evidence available in the real world, not on what wonderful things might happen in the near future. He doesn't get carried away by good times and is aware of the possibility of adversity: '... the buyer of insurance receives only a promise in exchange for his cash. The value of that promise should be appraised against the possibility of adversity, not prosperity.'[6]

Buffett's success at making money in significant doses doesn't distort his opinion of himself to the point where he feels he is God's gift to any business: '... we will not normally pay a lot in any purchase for what we are supposed to bring to the party – for we find that we don't ordinarily bring a lot.'[7]

He knows that he is merely a good investor and that it's his reliance on what he hasn't got – the skills of good business operators – that makes him rich. His modesty and humility make it possible for him not merely to know this, but also to comfortably embrace it.

CHAPTER SEVEN

Cutting your coat

'YOU DON'T HAVE TO BE AN EXPERT ON EVERY COMPANY, OR EVEN MANY; YOU ONLY HAVE TO BE ABLE TO EVALUATE COMPANIES WITHIN YOUR CIRCLE OF COMPETENCE.'[1] WB

THE HUMAN POTENTIAL Movement, which arose out of the social and intellectual milieu of the 1960s, spread the idea that 'we can do whatever we want if we try hard enough or spend enough time pursuing it.' This message has continued to gain ground in modern culture. It proposes that one need pay little heed to one's limitations as it's now possible to choose what you want to look like or be like with just a little help from a plastic surgeon, gym instructor, life coach or stockbroker.

This world view is reflected in the current wave of positive psychology propagated by Martin Seligman and others, who suggest that a positive attitude and other personality traits can be taught.

Even more sophisticated writers, such as Canadian journalist Malcolm Gladwell, fall into the trap. He implies in *Outliers*[2] that, along with opportunity, you need only 10,000 hours to become a genius. No doubt 10,000 hours will help, but it tends to imply that everyone can achieve anything if they put enough work in.

The effect is that modern individuals are frequently forced to live a highly pressured existence, in which cultural and internal demands remove any hope of peacefully living their own life with dignity and self-respect. This is a long way from the notion of living your life according to the resources available to you or, as the old idiom would have it: 'cutting one's coat according to one's cloth'.

We are accustomed to thinking of the resources referred to in this adage as material resources, but they certainly pertain to inner resources too. In this sense, the idea of cutting one's coat according to one's cloth suggests that each life is circumscribed by a range of factors; that, metaphorically speaking, each life is a cloth of a certain shape or size. Looking at Buffett's life, it would seem that his ability to embrace the parameters of his resources rather than strive to exceed their limits has borne fruit.

Accepting our inherent limits affords a sense of freedom and release from impossible pressure. The pressure to be or have what is not possible or what is not available additionally holds the danger of drawing us away from our available resources to 'elsewhere'. We could then end up starving at the banquet of our lives, rather than feasting on what is available.

The recommendation to cut one's coat according to one's cloth is not a defeatist instruction to diminish our own potential. It's more an invitation to grapple with our own reality; or a call to rely on our resources to create the kind of life we desire; one that is defined by the limits of who we are.

CHAPTER SEVEN

Buffett's understanding of himself, and what appears to be an easy acceptance of his strengths and weaknesses, allows him to find satisfaction in his own limits and capacities. It prevents him from desperately trying to succeed in areas that are not within his actual capacities or interests. He knows himself well enough to understand his areas of competence and his limitations and he's not seduced by any omnipotent notion that he can do everything.

It's a very complex and significant emotional achievement to know who we are; and not to slide into short-changing our sense of self or exaggerate our capacities. It sounds obvious to say we should be respectful of knowing who we are, but the slightest doubt can wreak havoc. Under these conditions, a timid and frightened view of the size of one's cloth can very easily result in shrunken and truncated aspirations that are not a true reflection of capacity.

Buffett's enormous achievements have not come from stretching himself beyond his limits, but rather the opposite. He has stayed in areas where he has a sense of competence and interest, deepened his understanding of them and conquered them. To be able to simply stay with something, and become increasingly familiar and competent is the opposite of 'doing everything'. Buffett has an ability to stay firmly in whatever patch he is working on. He is not distracted by an envious pre-occupation with lives and opportunities elsewhere, nor is he distracted by an inflated sense of self-importance leading him to be too good to look at the detail.

> 'If we have a strength, it is in recognising when we are operating well within our circle of competence and when we are approaching the perimeter. Predicting the long-term economics of companies that operate in fast-changing industries is simply far beyond our perimeter. If others claim predictive skill in

those industries – and seem to have their claims validated by the behaviour of the stock market – we neither envy nor emulate them. Instead, we just stick with what we understand. If we stray, we will have done so inadvertently, not because we got restless and substituted hope for rationality. Fortunately, it's almost certain that there will be opportunities from time to time for Berkshire to do well within the circle we've staked out.'[3] [That says it all.]

Buffett's understanding and acceptance of himself and the nature of his limits are reflected in the way he openly embraces his own particular style or prejudice:

> 'We will not follow the frequently prevalent approach of investing in securities where an attempt to anticipate market action overrides business valuations. Such so-called "fashion" investing has frequently produced very substantial and quick profits in recent years... It represents an investment technique whose soundness I can neither affirm nor deny. It does not completely satisfy my intellect (or perhaps my prejudices), and most definitely does not fit my temperament. I will not invest my own money based upon such an approach, hence I will most certainly not do so with your money. Finally, we will not seek out activity in investment operations, even if offering splendid profit expectations, where major human problems appear to have a substantial chance of developing.'[4]

This reflects the depth of Buffett's self-awareness and his capacity to know himself non-defensively and in a way that is non-idealising. He certainly doesn't have to distort the world or himself to justify what he does.

CHAPTER SEVEN

Buffett further reveals the acceptance of his limitations when he identifies with John Maynard Keynes' position:

> 'John Maynard Keynes, whose brilliance as a practising investor matched his brilliance in thought, wrote a letter to a business associate, F.C. Scott, on August 15, 1934, that says it all: "As time goes on, I get more and more convinced that the right method in investment is to put fairly large sums into enterprises which one thinks one knows something about and in management of which one thoroughly believes. It is a mistake to think that one limits one's risk by spreading too much between enterprises about which one knows little and has no reason for special confidence... One's knowledge and experience are definitely limited and there are seldom more than two or three enterprises at any given time in which I personally feel myself entitled to put full confidence."'[5]

Everything flows from Buffett's ability to constrain himself: 'I am likely to limit myself to things which are reasonably easy, safe, profitable and pleasant'.[6] Such limits! He limits himself to things he considers reasonably easy; things with which he is familiar and in which he has a keen interest. The result is that he is never weighed down by the anxiety and stress of mastering that which is too complex or not within his orbit.

The nature of his investments also prevents him from overstretching his emotional, intellectual and creative resources. He simply does not go into unsafe areas (even if hugely profitable) because it would betray who he is. And doing that would cost him emotionally, squandering resources that could be applied more profitably elsewhere.

For Buffett, like the psychoanalyst Donald Winnicott, 'good enough' is enough. This is worlds away from the kind of accomplishment required from a perfectionist or a narcissist, where nothing is ever enough. Buffett is just free to enjoy his life.

One could imagine having such an attitude if one lived a simple life with limited expenses doing things that are reasonably easy, safe, profitable and pleasant. Buffett, however, does this on the grandest scale imaginable, investing billions of dollars.

The limits Buffett can so easily set for himself aren't always truths or virtues in their own right. His capacity to set limits equally reflects a way of managing his own narrow interests and talents. Buffett has said many times:

> '... when management with a reputation for brilliance tackles a business with a reputation for bad economics, it is the reputation of the business that remains intact. I just wish I hadn't been so energetic in creating examples. My behaviour has matched that admitted by Mae West: "I was Snow White, but I drifted."'[7]

His conservatism is further revealed in his comments on what kinds of businesses he would be interested in investing in:

> '... experience, however, indicates that the best business returns are usually achieved by companies that are doing something quite similar today to what they were doing five or ten years ago... A business that constantly encounters major change also encounters many chances for major error. Furthermore, economic terrain that is forever shifting violently is ground on which it is difficult to build a fortress-like business franchise. Such a franchise is usually the key to sustained high returns... A far more serious problem occurs when the management of a great company gets side-tracked and neglects its wonderful base business while purchasing other businesses that are so-so or worse. When that happens, the suffering of investors is often

prolonged. Unfortunately, that is precisely what transpired years ago at both Coke and Gillette. (Would you believe that a few decades back they were growing shrimp at Coke and exploring for oil at Gillette?) Loss of focus is what most worries Charlie and me when we contemplate investing in businesses that in general look outstanding. All too often, we've seen value stagnate in the presence of hubris or of boredom that caused the attention of managers to wander. That's not going to happen again at Coke and Gillette, however – not given their current and prospective managements.'[8]

All of this hints that Buffett is not a man who relies on a great imagination and innovative foresight to provide investment opportunities for himself. That's who he is; that's his cloth. He thoroughly embraces his abilities, no matter how limited they may be. This is what cutting your coat is all about. It's not about a particular style – whether innovative or conservative. It is about applying your own resources in the most effective way.

CHAPTER EIGHT

Patience

'WHY SHOULD THE TIME REQUIRED FOR A PLANET TO CIRCLE THE SUN SYNCHRONISE PRECISELY WITH THE TIME REQUIRED FOR BUSINESS ACTIONS TO PAY OFF? INSTEAD, WE RECOMMEND NO LESS THAN A FIVE-YEAR TEST AS A ROUGH YARDSTICK OF ECONOMIC PERFORMANCE.' WB

THROUGHOUT HIS LIFE as an investor, time has been Buffett's best friend. His writings abound with quotes and stories on how, with compounding interest and time, the smallest amounts of money increase almost obscenely:

> 'Since the whole subject of compounding has such a crass ring to it, I will attempt to introduce a little class into the discussion by turning to the art world. Francis I of France paid 4000 ecus in 1540 for Leonardo da Vinci's *Mona Lisa*. On the off chance

CHAPTER EIGHT

that a few of you have not kept track of the fluctuations of the ecu, 4000 converted out to about $20,000. If Francis had kept his feet on the ground and he (and his trustees) had been able to find a six per cent after-tax investment, the estate now would be worth something over $1,000,000,000,000,000.00. That's $1 quadrillion or more than 3000 times the present national debt, all from six per cent. I trust this will end all discussion in our household about any purchase of paintings qualifying as an investment. However, as I pointed out last year, there are other morals to be drawn here. One is the wisdom of living a long time. The other impressive factor is the swing produced by relatively small changes in the rate of compound.'[1]

In embracing time as a business partner, the essential ingredient is patience - that deeply felt, contained space, devoid of urgency, where the relationship with the past makes it possible to have a calm anticipation of the future, without complaining or giving up.

Buffett fully understands the value of time, but admits that patience is not something that comes easily to him: 'We find doing nothing the most difficult task of all.'[2] Buffett does, however, structure his business activities and areas of engagement in such a way that makes it easier for him to be patient. He says:

'We are searching for operations that we believe are virtually certain to possess enormous competitive strength ten or twenty years from now. A fast-changing industry environment may offer the chance for huge wins, but it precludes the certainty we seek.'[3]

If you base your decisions on certainty and safety, it is much easier to be patient.

In addition to seeking certainty, he is also able to forgo the excitement of winning in the short term. Together, these qualities enable him to remain on course. He confirms this when he speaks of innovation:

> 'Fresh ideas, new products, innovative processes and the like cause our country's standard of living to rise, and that's clearly good. As investors, however, our reaction to a fermenting industry is much like our attitude toward space exploration: We applaud the endeavour but prefer to skip the ride.'[4]

He is explicitly contemptuous of activity as an investment strategy and in fact seems to believe that it is a costly mistake. He mocks the present-day attitude:

> 'Investment managers are even more hyperkinetic: their behaviour during trading hours makes whirling dervishes appear sedated by comparison. Indeed, the term "institutional investor" is becoming one of those self-contradictions called an oxymoron, comparable to "jumbo shrimp", "lady mudwrestler" and "inexpensive lawyer".'[5]

He drives home his point when he says:

> 'Berkshire, however, has a shareholder base – which it will have for decades to come – that has the longest investment horizon to be found in the public-company universe. Indeed, a majority of our shares are held by investors who expect to die still holding them. We can therefore ask our CEOs to manage for maximum long-term value, rather than for next quarter's earnings. We certainly don't ignore the current results of our businesses – in most cases, they are of great importance – but we never want

them to be achieved at the expense of our building ever-greater competitive strengths.'[6]

As one would expect, Buffett is very fond of the quote from the 17th-century French mathematician and philosopher Blaise Pascal: 'It has struck me that all men's misfortunes spring from the single cause that they are unable to stay quietly in one room.'[7]

He emphasises his respect for restraint on activity when he says:

> 'Our present setup unquestionably lets me devote a higher percentage of my time to thinking about the investment process than virtually anyone else in the money management business... and we continue to make more money when snoring than when active.'[8]

In an everyday world, and especially in an investment world, where 'action men' dominate, it is no mean feat to be patient. It requires a level of impulse control, which is quite uncommon. When speaking of persuasion, Al Capone suggests that a kind word is helpful but a kind word and a gun is more helpful. With a gun at our heads we can all manage what doesn't come easily. When the stakes are high enough, most of us can control our impulses and wait. Even a powerful animal with limited impulse control can sit almost frozen with patience when stalking its prey.

The question is: Is it Buffett's appetite for his prey that keeps his impulses in check, or is it a quality that runs deeper? Asked another way, does intense desire put a brake on his impulses so that he can achieve his goals? Or is it more than that?

Buffett may well have discovered that patience is a significant asset in his primary interest of making money. However, he seems to be naturally at ease with a more patient approach. There is some suggestion that his capacity for patience has strengthened over time, with his early investment style being characterised by an attraction to bargains and more active trading than his subsequent, and current, measured approach:

> 'Our goal is to find outstanding businesses at a sensible price, not a mediocre business at a bargain price. (It must be noted that your Chairman, always a quick study, required only twenty years to recognise how important it was to buy good businesses.)'[9]

Bargains are at an extreme. They are full of magical cheats and the exchange is seen as a 'steal', in which one triumphs in a smart way over someone else who is foolish. Landing a bargain seems to reflect one's specialness and perhaps Buffett's early focus on becoming a skilled bargain hunter gave him a certain confidence that he could make significant amounts of money. But as he matured, it became less necessary to add this magical thinking element to his style of investing.

One does not get the impression that Buffett exerts a great deal of control in maintaining his patient stance. He doesn't have Al Capone's metaphorical gun at his temple, forcing himself to do nothing.

Acquiring the calm containment required for unforced patience most likely relies on past experiences that have given us a confidence in our capacity to master the world; and a belief that things will, with time, more or less work out the way we hope, even if there is no guarantee. Past successes in managing the world would have confirmed the sense that patience, in light of our capacities, will bring something near to what we hope for and that disappointment will not be the usual outcome. Hope can facilitate a capacity to wait for the future to deliver but, over time, hope will need to combine with confidence and the repeated experience of success to stay alive. Without hope, everything

CHAPTER EIGHT

shrinks to the present; all needs and desires urgently press on the present for satisfaction.

One way of dealing with urgently pressing desires is to diminish their worth, much in the way the fox who desired the grapes did in one of Aesop's fables. Here, the fox, after agitatedly and desperately jumping up against the wall to reach some rather delicious looking grapes, walks away saying to himself 'they are probably sour anyway'. He diminishes the compelling attractiveness of the object of desire and is therefore free from the pressure to obtain it.

Buffett's patience does not seem to come through any denial of desire, which would, after all, make it easy to not be pressured to achieve something because one had no 'investment' in the outcome. This patience is based on the 'skirting around' or 'giving up' of the pressures of desire in order to easily be patient and therefore have no inner urgency. However, Buffett's patience lives happily with an intense desire to make a lot of money. He has not given up on desire at all.

Buffett's intense life-long desire to acquire money lacks a frantic or excited quality. He seems to approach his task with a quiet inner confidence. This allows him the patience to think clearly and calmly over time about the decisions that he needs to make, with a lively interest in what he is doing but without agitating pressure.

Perhaps what helps Buffett sustain calmness is his realistic attitude about the nature of how long it takes to achieve certain goals and how complex the path to achieve them may be. He states the obvious with more than obvious implications: 'No matter how great the talent or effort, some things just take time: you can't produce a baby in one month by getting nine women pregnant.'[10]

He again makes uncommon common sense: 'After all, why should the time required for a planet to circle the sun synchronise precisely with the time required for business actions to pay off? Instead, we recommend no less than a five-year test as a rough yardstick of economic performance.'[11]

What is unusual about Buffett is that when the world panics and is driven to mindless action, he retreats to an inner space where he evaluates the confusing pessimistic moments and makes his decisions patiently, in his own time. He does not live in fear of disaster or of missing out. The world for him seems boundlessly fruitful and if he misses out now he seems to have the confidence that life will present further opportunities.

CHAPTER NINE

Deferring gratification

'THERE'S MUCH TO BE SAID FOR JUST PUTTING ONE FOOT IN FRONT OF THE OTHER EVERY DAY.' WB

WE ARE ALL familiar with the story of the Three Little Pigs. Here, in this tale of maturity and impulse control, the first and second little pigs spend most of their time doing what children do best: play. They take their adult responsibilities, which would force them to defer the pleasure to be gained from playing, lightly. They rapidly and half-heartedly assemble dwellings made of straw, for the one, and sticks, for the other. Meanwhile, the third little pig, who seems less fun, but who represents maturity in the story, spends his time building a protective haven for all of them (the house of bricks). He no doubt has just as hearty an appetite for fun as his brothers. However, his capacity to put off having fun is what sets him apart in both maturity and his capacity to manage the challenges of the world (or the wolf).

The very word *investing* implies that what one engages with now is integrally tied to the future, and that the fruits of the present labour are perhaps not going to be immediate. To choose investing as a way of making a living requires a capacity for deferring gratification. Investors, like the third little pig, need to work hard now with the view to benefit, not immediately but in the future – even at the cost of immediate pleasure. In Buffett's words, investing is 'forgoing consumption now in order to have the ability to consume more at a later date'. If you want to be a successful investor there is no question that you have to have the qualities of the third little pig.

For Buffett, it's not a simple matter of deferring gratification or not. He seems to have a significant capacity to defer gratification over long periods of time. Prices can fluctuate quite wildly over short periods of time with a gamut of emotions driving people to buy and sell various businesses. Beyond his capacity to make astute judgements of value in the first instance, it is his ability to hold things over long periods of time that makes it possible for him to allow the more accurate value of these businesses to reveal themselves.

We begin life as a bundle of impulses and pressing needs that at first seem impossible to ignore. If we are lucky, we mature and move to a position where we can defer immediate satisfaction for long-term goals, such as forgoing certain environmentally damaging pleasures in the interest of protecting our planet a hundred years from now; or curtailing current expenditure to secure the financial future of generations not yet born.

Freud's constructs of the 'id', 'ego' and 'super ego' are illuminating metaphors for understanding the force that powers the desire for gratification. The id is a wild, impulse-ridden, rampant drive to have one's needs met immediately. It has no restraint and no concern for anything other than immediate gratification. It is like a greedy, out-

CHAPTER NINE

of-control animal meeting its needs wherever it can without concern for anyone or anything. It is desire gone mad.

At the other extreme, the super ego is the perfectionistic, moralistic representation of the highest social values, demanding a pure, perfect, blemish-free life. It is God to the id's Devil.

The ego in this model is given the daunting task of reconciling these extreme dimensions of the mind. For example, the ego would prefer when one is hungry that one doesn't smash the window of the bakery, grab the pastries and stuff them in one's mouth. The ego prefers that one get a job, earn some money, go to the bakery during opening hours and exchange the money for the pastries to satisfy one's hunger. It has the additional task of managing the puritanical, demanding super ego (conscience) that can be equally relentless in its demands, suggesting: 'what do you think you are doing eating pastries, you disgusting, pathetic, fat slob? Didn't you see yourself in the mirror last night?' The ego having already compromised with the id must now make peace with the super ego and perhaps order a salad roll.

Freud's model is a useful illustration of the dynamics that take place and the maturity that is required to have any capacity at all to defer gratification. And from this it is obvious that Buffett has a strong ego, which allows him to deal with conflict quite calmly. He clearly isn't oppressed by a persecutory super ego that lashes out at him when disappointed in his lack of immediate success. Equally, he is not pulled this way and that by an impulse-ridden id wanting all its needs met immediately. To be able to function as Buffett does calls for a particularly strong ego to manage the emergence of desperateness.

Desperateness is a trait that seems to steal away from time and space. Desperateness seems to feed off urgency and impairs judgement; it distorts and obliterates the more mature and softer elements of the personality. It strips things down to a base need to quieten whatever one is desperate for. There is no time and space for mature thought or a capacity to think through the consequences of the immediate action. When desperate, there is a fear of losing or missing out.

Desperateness seems to emerge in the presence of extreme internal pressures that are experienced as unavoidable. These needs turn to and focus on a hyper-valued object, whose value is either real (as in the case of a starving person wanting a cup of rice) or displaced, as there could be with a certain kind of wealthy man who is still desperate in his wish to make more money.

Once stimulated, there can be enormous excitement in the light of the promise of the satisfaction of this elusive desire. The smell of satisfaction that feeds the excitement and urgency creates something close to a state of emergency, where the object of the desperateness is pursued in a relentlessly single-minded manner. This obscures from awareness the need for restraint and the threat of danger to others or oneself. The blindness created by the majesty of the promise carries one above and away from the mundane, dragging impact of sound judgement. Woe betide anyone or anything that stands in the path of the promise.

Buffett's strength of ego allows him to manage levels of excitement and vital engagement in an intense life of investing without ever being swept away by desperateness. Few individuals are able to manage this.

To avoid being desperate and to defer gratification, one must be able to contain anxiety. Containing anxiety is about a capacity to hold fears and anxieties in a space inside oneself without attempting to destroy, displace or deny them with action. It's a capacity to survive uncertainty without premature foreclosure or control. It's a space where one can survive not knowing what the answer is; where one doesn't know how to get out of some sort of trouble; and where you can endure the existence of the anxiety while the future reveals the

CHAPTER NINE

answer. When anxiety is well contained, there is an ability to not fragment, go to pieces, panic or get desperate or, most especially, the ability not to invoke a range of defences against the anxiety.

Defending against anxiety in the way that people traditionally do is very different from containing anxiety. When anxiety is contained, there's a manageable awareness of the anxiety and an understanding of the reasons why one is anxious. This leaves one open to take those concerns into account and make a clearer and better-informed judgement. This seems to be Buffett's way. The alternative to containing anxiety is to invoke defences against it. Here the anxiety is not experienced consciously or held in the mind but transformed into such things as physical symptoms, frantic activity or avoidance of certain situations. The full complexity of the anxiety-provoking situation is distorted to accommodate self-deception and to avoid feeling the anxiety.

Containing anxiety is one of the essential components of an ability to defer gratification. The other elements of emotional maturity that seem to be strongly supportive of a capacity to defer gratification are a lack of desperateness and a strong ego. These elements all combine in Buffett to facilitate his investment style, and without them and the way they come together, the emotional demands that his investment style put on him would be impossible. This dynamic is reflected in his refrain that:

> 'Intelligent expansion or acquisition opportunities... are most likely to pop up when conditions in the debt market are clearly oppressive. Our basic principle is that, if you want to shoot rare, fast-moving elephants, you should always carry a loaded gun.'[1]

This reveals his preparedness to frustrate the wish to get the highest returns on his money at all times in order to wait until the elephant walks past. When the debt market is oppressive, it is very difficult to access debt to make acquisitions. One therefore has to be holding cash for this purpose, which generally implies a lower return than if fully invested. Buffett's mature down-to-earth way of being, especially when viewed against others who invest large sums of money, is well captured when he advises that: 'There's much to be said for just putting one foot in front of the other every day.'[2]

Putting one foot in front of the other, in a steady unrushed way can lead to significant financial advantages, and happens to have an important mathematical edge over a more frenzied approach. Buffett looks at an extreme example:

> 'Imagine that Berkshire had only $1, which we put in a security that doubled by year end and was then sold. Imagine further that we used after-tax proceeds to repeat this process in each of the next nineteen years, scoring a double each time. At the end of the twenty years, the 34 per cent capital gains tax that we would have paid on the profits from each sale would have delivered about $13,000 to the government and we would be left with about $25,250. Not bad. If, however, we made a single fantastic investment that itself doubled twenty times during the twenty years, our dollar would grow to $1,048,576. Were we then to cash out, we would pay a 34 per cent tax of roughly $356,500 and be left with about $692,000.'[3]

It's clear that to win over impulsiveness, major hurdles need to be surmounted and major personal qualities need to be in place. If these qualities aren't in place, they will certainly be starkly revealed in a situation where there is a dramatic rising or falling of prices. Such a situation commonly stirs up desperateness, uncontained anxiety and impulsive decision-making, particularly when large amounts of

CHAPTER NINE

money are involved. However, Buffett's capacity to contain anxiety and defer gratification come together nicely in his counter-intuitive response to the event of falling market prices: 'If the business continues to satisfy us, we welcome lower market prices of stocks we own as an opportunity to acquire even more of a good thing at a better price.'[4]

Buffett doesn't panic.

CHAPTER TEN

Frugality

'WHEN WE WERE DUE TO CLOSE THE PURCHASE AT CHARLIE'S OFFICE, JACK WAS LATE. FINALLY ARRIVING, HE EXPLAINED THAT HE HAD BEEN DRIVING AROUND LOOKING FOR A PARKING METER WITH SOME UNEXPIRED TIME. THAT WAS A MAGIC MOMENT FOR ME. I KNEW THEN THAT JACK WAS GOING TO BE MY KIND OF MANAGER.'[1] WB

DOES ONE HAVE to be frugal to become extremely wealthy? And is it so that counting one's pennies enables the pounds to look after themselves? One thing is for sure, as penny pinchers go, Buffett is up there with the best.

Being frugal is the opposite extreme of indulging one's impulses, and is different from temperance, which requires finding a balance between meeting our needs and denying them. Frugality is an extreme position that says no to impulses and the desire for satisfaction.

CHAPTER TEN

It is not about restraining impulses, but rather about denying them. Here restraint gets a life of its own, and not necessarily a better life. James Griffin[2] suggests that frugality is not an ultimate good or virtue in itself, but it may be instrumental in bringing one closer to the things that are virtuous or of intrinsic value. Depending on how it's used, it can be in the service of good or misery.

It may be that frugality is generally seen as particularly virtuous because the restraint involved is so much more reassuring and appealing than the picture of out-of-control indulgence. But if one is to look at self-denial as a virtue in itself, rather than something that can bring one closer to what is really important in life, it is hard to imagine how, say, having sex, a piece of cake or a holiday once every sixteen years is going to bring about a better life. Denial itself is not an ultimate virtue; it's an essential component of a mature life, used temperately.

However, frugality is complex in its dimensions. For instance, does frugality necessarily imply denial? Is one frugal only because one chooses not to enjoy the resources to which one has access? Can one be completely self-indulgent by being frugal?

When Buffett is excited by finding a man whom he feels is his kind of man - a man who arrives late for a meeting because he is driving around looking for an unexpired parking meter - he is not looking at a man who is denying himself. He is looking at a man who is completely indulging himself in what matters to him, which is saving money.

The parking meter man's apparent frugality is seen as a virtue by Buffett in symbolic form only, because it is nothing about actually saving real money. A businessman of that stature can make much more money with fifteen minutes of his time than he can by saving a dime on a parking meter. This is about a whole way of being. It is about the value of money being woven into his personality structure and his understanding of what really matters in life.

Buffett and many other people idealise not spending money, almost for its own sake. But perhaps it is for the sake of, or it feels like it's for the sake of, leaving more money to accumulate. Of course, in this case the idealisation of not spending a dime may, in real financial terms, cost more than the saving. Ultimately, however, Buffett's attraction to these people who are frugal, specifically in terms of not wanting to spend money, is a winner for him. They are the sort of people who, when working in his businesses, would avoid the unnecessary expenditure of money, thereby helping him achieve his ultimate goal of accumulating as much capital as possible. In the end, the kind of so-called frugality that we are looking at in Buffett is not particularly about self-denial, but rather a dedication to not spending money unnecessarily, so that it can be accumulated.

For some people this emotional over-investment in not spending can become extremely destructive because it restricts them to the extent that they can't use their money creatively to make more money. This, however, is certainly not the case with Buffett.

As suggested in *Love*, for Buffett the ultimate motivation in life comes from the acquisition and accumulation of money, which prevents extreme frugality in relation to money from becoming too high a price to pay. In fact, it's no price to pay at all because, while denying himself the pleasure of what money can bring, he is only adding to the ultimate pleasure: accumulating more by compounding the growth of the money that would otherwise have been spent in pursuit of short-term satisfaction.

Frugality for Buffett seems an over-invested, deeply reassuring, symbolic act. It seems to make him feel good to know that people are not over-indulging. But more than this, Buffett's aim to accumulate as much money as he can, makes him a collector, like any other. Stamp collectors and coin collectors accumulate their loved objects for the simple joy of knowing that they own them, not because they want to use the stamps to send letters or the coins to buy the objects of their desire. Their enjoyment comes from cherishing the possession of the object. If the valued object is money, which also happens to be the means of trade in everyday existence, then a deeply frugal attitude towards spending it is the same as that of the collector who wants to treasure and not consume.

It's interesting that the restraint involved in frugality is available to Buffett on many levels. It facilitates a mature, measured attitude toward investing that has been extremely helpful in making him so successful.

The thrill, excitement and love of life that's obvious in the collector's energetic pursuit of the objects of his desire reveal the way in which much more powerful energies have been sublimated into the collecting impulse. Freud suggests, with the term sublimation, that primitive, deeply felt impulses are transformed into higher forms of wishes and desires, such as artistic creations or intellectual pursuits. It may be that Buffett's singular focus on accumulating money contains, in a sublimated form, a connection to such powerful parts of his emotional life that being frugal in order to accumulate money is gratifying significant and deeply felt needs.

CHAPTER ELEVEN

Conscience

'AGONISING OVER ERRORS IS A MISTAKE, BUT ACKNOWLEDGING AND ANALYSING THEM CAN BE USEFUL, THOUGH THAT PRACTICE IS RARE IN CORPORATE BOARDROOMS.' WB

BUFFETT THINKS AND acts without anxious constraint, but with thoughtful measuredness. Despite the daunting implications of the decisions he makes, he is not afraid of making them. He acts on his own considered and researched judgement. This ability of his is in no small part due to the way he judges himself in regard to his successes and failures – the structure of his conscience. While he has strict boundaries for what he will and won't let himself do, he displays a generosity of spirit towards himself when he errs.

Winston Churchill suggests that 'success is about going from failure to failure without loss of enthusiasm'. He is speaking here of a very

CHAPTER ELEVEN

special and complex quality that is not easily available to us. Most of us are endowed with an internal judging faculty - a conscience - which is usually very quick to punish when we fail at something important. Certain individuals are particularly vulnerable to this kind of punitive conscience. Their feelings of inadequacy or being bad are very close to the surface and much energy is expended in appeasing the punitive conscience.

This is epitomised in its extreme form in a person with obsessive-compulsive tendencies. Such individuals are constantly anxious and fearful about internal punishments from their conscience for not doing the 'right thing'. It results in them becoming driven to be productive and good at all times, tyrannising their lives with rules, lists, rigid and inflexible beliefs, extreme conscientiousness and general perfectionism. This type of personality has almost zero tolerance for making mistakes. The ruthless, critical eye of the punitive conscience severely curtails the person's capacity to think and be creative or free. There is little hope of this individual taking Winston Churchill's advice. And there is little hope of this individual being a Buffett.

At the other extreme, the freedom to go from failure to failure is readily available to the opposite personality type - the psychopath. This kind of person is not plagued by any sense that he is bad, however bad he might actually be. Bad is his thing. His controlling conscience is almost non-existent. He lacks the capacity for self-criticism and self-reflection. His ambitions, behaviour and understanding of his capacities are not measured and controlled by an overarching judging faculty. Instead, they are indulged. This individual is therefore vulnerable to grandiose thought and action and an over-developed belief in his ability. A small amount of success will rapidly lead to him believing he has the Midas touch. His decisions are based on his belief that he is fabulous. He is not inhibited by too much boring detail when making decisions. The psychopath's impulses tend to run the show, unfettered by anxiety and guilt. He is not constricted by the fear of making mistakes and failing, as is the obsessive compulsive. For this individual, the road ahead is a minefield – the mines are just different. And he is equally far away from being a Buffett.

If a person achieves maturity, as most of us do, life is lived in-between these extremes. Here, we are neither incapacitated by inaction nor by mindless uninhibited action. As with many other difficult-to-balance parts of life, Buffett straddles this divide exquisitely. In fact he seems to have the perfect measure of freedom and constraint.

Having a sympathetic conscience allows one to take seriously the making of important decisions; and to recover from mistakes without attacking oneself too viciously for failing. The sympathetic conscience provides the balance between freedom and constraint. It means having the freedom to act in the best way one can at the time without being disabled by a fear of making mistakes or by some sense that mistakes can't be survived. It suggests an understanding that mistakes are made and that, while one might not be able to go back and totally repair the damage, one need not fall into despair and hopelessness, because it may be possible to make up for the mistake in the future. Failing this, one can mourn the loss of what is spoiled without indulging in self-annihilating recriminations.

Buffett himself seems to have a conscience that is similar to what Goldilocks was looking for and found in baby bear's porridge: 'Not too hot, not too cold, just right'. We could say he has the 'Goldilocks dose' of conscience.

The particular nature of his conscience is in fact a necessary condition for his greatness as an investor. It constrains him from self-indulgent, impulsive decision-making on the one hand; and frees him from excessive self-flagellation for mistakes he makes on the other.

CHAPTER ELEVEN

This allows him to make sound judgements and act on them with the freedom implied in Churchill's quote.

Buffett, however, has a very strong, inhibiting, ruthlessly crushing conscience when he begins to act outside his area of safety – it just won't let him go there. Buffett won't get involved in major allocations of capital unless his well-developed criteria lead him to believe that a sound investment is being made. While initially he will completely avoid anything that doesn't meet his standards, his level of punitive conscience seems not to be brought to bear if he stays within his circle of competence. If a well-considered decision turns out to be a big mistake, he will be able to learn from it and continue to do his work. He will not become extremely anxious or depressed; nor will he try to avert action in the future to avoid the punishment of an over-active conscience. Buffett's more sympathetic and generous conscience is revealed when he speaks so refreshingly about his errors:

> 'Our Vice Chairman, Charlie Munger, has always emphasised the study of mistakes rather than successes, both in business and other aspects of life. He does so in the spirit of the man who said: "All I want to know is where I'm going to die so I'll never go there." You'll immediately see why we make a good team: Charlie likes to study errors and I have generated ample material for him, particularly in our textile and insurance businesses.'[1]

He continues to reveal his healthy conscience when he says: 'Agonising over errors is a mistake, but acknowledging and analysing them can be useful, though that practice is rare in corporate boardrooms.'[2]

Throughout Buffett's writing it's clear that he is quite unlike the cat in Mark Twain's famous aphorism: The cat, having sat upon a hot stove lid, will not sit upon a hot stove lid again. But he won't sit upon a cold stove lid, either.

For Buffett there seems to be a level of contentment in himself and his expectations so that when he disappoints himself, he doesn't feel crushed. His self-esteem is such that he doesn't feel that he has to prove that he is clever or that he is infallible, which is why he allows himself to be fallible. Buffett is simply getting on with the job of making money, not the job of managing his self-esteem. He's not really that interested in how his actions reflect on him as a clever man; he is just interested in how his actions reflect on increasing his net worth over time.

Buffett's friendly relationship with his conscience allows him the freedom to be so charming and refreshingly honest about his fallibility. He is able to describe himself in self-deprecating terms with great ease and without ever having to resort to defensiveness: 'If the physiological rules that applied to Pinocchio were to apply to me, my nose would now draw crowds.'[3]

It's hard to find a complete explanation for Buffett's generous conscience, but perhaps some clues can be found in the nature of his relationship with himself. He lives quite self-respectfully. He works hard according to his own standard, does the right thing by himself and lives with the mistakes he makes.

CHAPTER TWELVE

Greed

'MAE WEST HAD IT RIGHT: "TOO MUCH OF A GOOD THING CAN BE WONDERFUL."'[1] WB

BUFFETT'S INSATIABLE APPETITE for making money necessarily forces one to ask whether he is a greedy man. But then, what is greed? Is it an appetite that can't be satisfied – a certain kind of insatiability? Or is it a pejorative label attached to an appetite that some would consider excessive. If so, what's wrong with having an excessive appetite? Why shouldn't we be free to have as much as we want, particularly if it's not harming anyone else?

In the 1987 Oliver Stone film *Wall Street* the character Gordon Gekko says: 'Greed... is good. Greed is right, greed works. Greed clarifies, cuts through, and captures the essence of the evolutionary spirit. Greed, in all of its forms - greed for life, for money, for love, for knowledge - has marked the upward surge of mankind.' This sentiment reflects that of the infamous investor and financier Ivan Boesky (arguably the man on whom the Gordon Gekko character is based), in his commencement address to the School of Business Administration at UC Berkeley, when he said: 'Greed is all right, by the way. I want you to know that. I think greed is healthy. You can be greedy and still feel good about yourself'.

If we regard greed as a deep, relentless desire for something that can never be satisfied, we would be hard pressed to differentiate it from the insatiability of life itself. Being alive means always yearning deeply for something: food, sleep, peace and quiet, affection, satisfaction at work, sex and leisure. But is it greed? Or, does greed imply more than just insatiability?

In a world of liberal democracies is greed not possibly even good, as the *Wall Street* film suggests? Isn't it basically the founding notion of capitalism? Isn't it necessary to create and acquire goods beyond those one 'needs' to create surplus capital and, consequently, economic growth? And even if we discount capitalism, don't we need to create surpluses for our future survival? If we do, and if the healthy generation of surpluses is helpful, why do we call it greed?

The concept of greed seems to enter into formal thought around the fourth century, when the monk Evagrius Ponticus[2] listed eight evil thoughts. These were later formalised by Pope Gregory I as the Seven Deadly Sins, of which greed was one. The influential philosopher and theologian Saint Augustine included greed in his discussion of immorality, referring to it as *avaritia* (wanting more than is enough), which he saw as the root of all evil. Etymologically, *avaritia* refers more to a forcefulness of yearning than to the object of greed. Greed's pejorative flavour seemed to emerge from the dynamic where the forcefulness of yearning took up so much space in the mind of the greedy that it interfered with a full devotion of one's energies to God. During the early Middle Ages the ascetic ideal was strong and the idea of acquiring possessions was spurned, not so much in the name of virtue as in the belief that worldly concerns could divert one's attention from higher spiritual pursuits. This made greed a serious vice and threat to the meaning of life at the time. By the time the Renaissance had taken hold, though, there seemed to be less certainty about the absolute evil of greed. Poggio Bracciolini, the Italian scholar, writer and humanist, in his 1429 dialogue *On Avarice*, quotes fellow humanist Antonio Loschi's more kindly and utilitarian attitude toward greed in the service of business investment, the growing of cities, philanthropy and wage earning: '... it's obvious that avarice is not only natural, it is useful and necessary in human beings, for it teaches them to provide for themselves those things that are necessary for sustaining the frailty of human nature and for avoiding inconveniences.'[3]

The course of history seems to indicate that greed will never sit in an uncomplicated place in our minds. As recently as 1967, the Indian mystic and spiritual master Meher Baba described greed as: '... a state of restlessness of the heart, and it consists mainly of craving for power and possessions. Possessions and power are sought for the fulfilment of desires. Man is only partially satisfied in his attempt to have the fulfilment of his desires, and this partial satisfaction fans and increases the flame of craving instead of extinguishing it. Thus greed always finds an endless field of conquest and leaves the man endlessly dissatisfied.'[4]

Despite the doubts about the legitimacy of greed as a real phenomenon and despite its cultural and historical complexity, we all have an intuitive grasp of greed as a real experience in ourselves and in others. Greed has its beginnings in ordinary desire and appetite, but it's a long way from a healthy appetite.

Greed is a mutation of appetite. Appetite is the desire that constantly keeps us connected to life, engaged with the world and seeking satisfaction. Appetite can be satisfied. It looks for what it wants and if it can't find exactly what it wants, it finds something close enough and makes do.[5] If, however, certain internal forces begin to put pressure on appetite, a mutation occurs where appetite increases dramatically and often unendingly to the point where satisfaction is almost impossible.

Greed is a relentless, desperate, *absolutely* insatiable desire or yearning to acquire or possess more, only for oneself. The malady of greed is one where satisfaction and contentment elude. The greedy impulse that torments relentlessly can't, for any significant period of time, make do. It can't appreciate what it has, because what it has is never enough; it always wants more. Everything that it has is in some way disappointing, corroded or tarnished.

The afflicted individual may pursue his interests with great passion; but when he gets what he thinks he wants, he seems to be robbed of satisfaction and contentment.

This affliction can be exacerbated by envy and its characteristic style of seeing good only in what others have, thus preventing the possession from soothing its acquirer. With envy there is often a scooping out of the worth of what one has; and seeing this worth only elsewhere – even if it is very similar to one's own. One's own good qualities are often not recognised as having any value and yet are yearned for with a desperate longing when seen in others.

It is even worse when the individual loathes himself and his own qualities. This dynamic removes any satisfaction from the acquisition of what's really longed for because once what is longed for becomes one's own, it gets tarnished and destroyed by the very loathing for all that one is and has. The only real good one can see lies in someone else's life. The stage is perfectly set here for insatiable greed.

Any form of tarnishing of what one has, not only envy, can lead to an unappeasable appetite. In cases such as these, the extreme longing can't make do with the kind of partial satisfaction that can provide some contentment.

It's this tendency to have one's acquisitions devalued by tarnishing that characterises the miserably greedy, and this is where they depart from the cheerfully greedy. The cheerfully greedy appreciate and value what they get. Each batch of acquisitions seems to provide some satisfaction. For the cheerfully greedy there is a capacity to make do with the fulfilment of each demand, even if it's not entirely complete; and there is a sense of gratitude for everything they have. There is a freedom from the kind of self-importance that leads to contemptuous pickiness; and there is an ability to enjoy what one gets. The cheerfully greedy just want more of a good thing. They want to build it up layer upon layer. This is Buffett.

So it seems that it's not the forcefulness of the yearning that torments, but the lack of being able to value what you have. If you can enjoy what you have, no amount of wanting more seems to be able to spoil it: unless the pressure for larger and larger amounts reduces your capacity to delight in what you have; and unless the need for more and more devalues what is yearned for and causes you to focus entirely on the chase.

For the miserably greedy, there is a bottomless pit that can never be filled. But, while Buffett also never seems able to fill his pit, it's not bottomless. It's just very deep, filled with highly valued possessions. This makes Buffett feel happy and filled up, as opposed to the miserably greedy, who feel empty and desperate.

This cheerful, non-agitated, non-tormented nature of his greed is a completely necessary condition for Buffett to be Buffett: a man who is calm, who can be patient, can think clearly, is not overly prone to desperate neediness; but also a man who must continue acquiring more and more money.

Some might argue that Buffett's focus on making more and more money might have shrunk his openness to other dimensions of life. But then this is true of any passion or intense pursuit that requires a large amount of energy and time. This is after all the complaint that St Augustine had about greed: it interfered with the full devotion of one's energies to God.

Perhaps nothing much has changed in our attitude toward greed since St Augustine's time. Perhaps all that has changed is the cultural context of what we see as God. In modern times, the God that one is expected to devote one's energies toward would more likely be a balanced life in pursuit of happiness, and it is perhaps here that greed may get its modern pejorative slant. An intensely focused individual would today be implored to broaden his focus to a full enjoyment of the complexities of life, rather than to obtain all his satisfactions by intense devotion to one dimension of life.

Is greed in the end just a value judgement about what makes a good life? And is it greed's one-dimensional focus that gives it a reputation for being unhelpful in achieving a good life?

Buffett seems to have woven so much of his good life into the service of making money that it's not easy to see what compromises he has made. That may be the job of those closer to him.

CHAPTER THIRTEEN

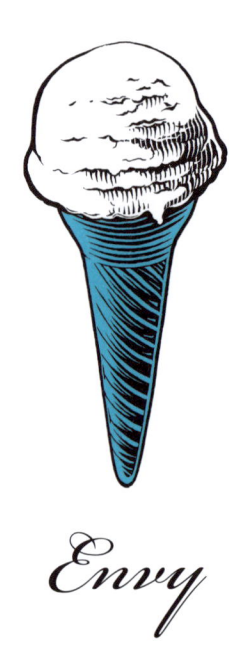

Envy

'FOR ME, RONALD REAGAN HAD IT RIGHT: "IT'S PROBABLY TRUE THAT HARD WORK NEVER KILLED ANYONE, BUT WHY TAKE THE CHANCE?".' WB

AS HUMANS WE have a disposition for choosiness and a bent for making selections. We don't just accept all that is there for us or all that is offered to us. We choose what is most desirable from the available possibilities. And, while this is a natural part of the human condition, it is also this that sows the first seeds for the development of envy.[1]

When envy is stirred up, an over-sensitive interest in what is 'elsewhere' develops. The 'elsewhere' is not just looked at out of innocuous curiosity, it is the beginning of a comparison of ourselves with others; a comparison in which we are not simply making distinctions, but distinctions that are laden with judgement. We find that 'something is always preferable to something else'.[2] Furthermore, given that we live in a social context, what we choose becomes very vulnerable to what we see others choosing, particularly those people whom we admire and wish to emulate. We therefore become exposed to the impressiveness of people around us and vulnerable to their views. And this, in turn, can lead us to lose our internal scorecard – something that has proven to be one of Buffett's most valuable assets.

This way of being, with an internal scorecard, is the opposite of envy. It allows one to stay in one's own skin, to evaluate received wisdom with clarity and to make one's own judgements from a solid, independent base.

Envy is stimulated by a disappointment with the self – a sense that one is lacking in some way and that all the good exists outside oneself. The good is removed from the self and transferred to the thing or person one envies; and this thing or person becomes the container of all that is desirable.

The envious individual is therefore unable to take Freud's advice, which suggests, 'One should never let better stand in the way of good'. Instead, there is always a feeling of disappointment and the experience of the perfectly good being overshadowed by the alluringly irresistible, the 'something better'.

Imagine, as a child, walking into one of those tantalising, brightly lit ice-cream shops. The shiny glass counters and wall-to-wall flavours are forever intertwined in your memory with that unforgettable smell of bliss. Once you subdue your desire to have it all, you fix on one or two flavours. Then the treacherous moment arrives, before you even realise it. You want just a tiny taste of your friend's ice-cream, and it's nicer than yours! Once this is discovered and even before, when you are asking for the taste, you are beginning to lose the sense of ownership and delight in your own ice-cream. It is now tarnished by not being something else, despite the fact that it would have been a perfectly

CHAPTER THIRTEEN

wonderful experience if you had not looked elsewhere. The good has been vanquished by the desire for something better. To spoil it, all you need to think is, 'I wish I'd got the chocolate', and your cookies-and-cream will never be the same. Envy is the ultimate spoiler.

If one isn't able to hold on to and value the good one has, then that good is vulnerable to being frivolously passed over in the mind for something 'better'. In this way, we are then always led away from what we have: the chocolate soon loses its attraction and is replaced by strawberry, and on it goes.

As an investor, Buffett relies centrally on his capacity to be his own man; to make considered judgements from the place of an internal scorecard, separate from the crowd, where he is not concerned with the views and actions of the majority. He lives in a contained, separate, independent world that is the opposite of the envious position.

Buffett is not plagued by the sense of self-deficiency and lacking that those experiencing envy are. He doesn't have a desired, envisioned self that is unreachable. He doesn't wish to be some imposing person that he isn't; nor does he long for the impressive qualities of others that he doesn't have.

In a more down-to-earth way, he absorbs, digests and integrates the qualities he admires in people such as, say, Benjamin Graham, instead of idealising them. And because he doesn't take them into himself, he can let them be their substantial selves while still drawing strength from their presence.

Buffett goes after what he wants, feels he can get it, and does get it. But he also knows what he can't get, and does not yearn for it. For instance, we know he is really fond of making money, preferably in large quantities. Yet, he went through the whole dot-com boom watching others make obscene amounts of money, without being tempted to join the gold rush, because he knew he couldn't do it.

Buffett doesn't feel the kind of lack many of us are prone to; he has a realistic acceptance of himself and his own limits, he knows that he is just Warren Buffett; he is not George Soros or Julian Robertson or Donald Trump. The freedom this gives him to live in his own world and focus on the tasks at hand is immeasurable. It sets him apart from the rest of us who spend large amounts of mental energy consumed by our fascination with rivals and those we perceive to be better than us. It gives him exceptional focus in a world filled with distractions.

Buffett's sincere admiration for others is eloquently portrayed when he says:

> 'In fairness, we've seen plenty of successes as well, some truly outstanding. There are many giant company managers whom I greatly admire; Ken Chenault of American Express, Jeff Immelt of G.E. and Dick Kovacevich of Wells Fargo come quickly to mind. But I don't think I could do the management job they do. And I know I wouldn't enjoy many of the duties that come with their positions – meetings, speeches, foreign travel, the charity circuit and governmental relations. For me, Ronald Reagan had it right: "It's probably true that hard work never killed anyone – but why take the chance?"
>
> So I've taken the easy route, just sitting back and working through great managers who run their own shows. My only tasks are to cheer them on, sculpt and harden our corporate culture, and make major capital-allocation decisions. Our managers have returned this trust by working hard and effectively...'[3]

One could say that the antidote to envy is an ability to celebrate the strengths of others. Buffett does this with absolute ease; and he does more than simply celebrate them. He is able to draw on them to benefit himself, without any need to cut them down to size. And then he goes

CHAPTER THIRTEEN

beyond leaving them intact; he actually protects and encourages them to be better than himself and leaves them free to be themselves. He is not enviously entangled with them, so he is free from the relentless inner torment of only being good and not better. Buffett knows he is not them, doesn't want to be them, and is delighted to have them there. His sense of self is protected by a thick membrane and he stays within his skin with all his strengths and limitations.

Not only does Buffett realise that, as Harold Coffin says, 'Envy is the art of counting the other fellow's blessings instead of your own',[4] he is well aware that his capacity to spot and harness the significant blessings of others is the source of much of his success.

CHAPTER FOURTEEN

Narcissism

'WHY SEARCH FOR A NEEDLE BURIED IN A HAYSTACK WHEN ONE IS SITTING IN PLAIN SIGHT?' WB

NARCISSISM ISN'T EXACTLY a term that one would associate with Buffett. Indeed, one of his most striking features is an unusual *lack* of narcissism. But this unusual lack is so centrally part of him that it is not just an absence we are looking at; Buffett's lack of narcissism is an active description of who he is and it's what makes him stand out from others.

One of the main reasons why Buffett is such a unique individual, and why so few of us can do what Buffett can do, is that we are all narcissistically affected by the upheavals of growing up. This doesn't imply that everyone has a narcissistic personality or that only extreme forms of narcissism are disruptive. It implies that even our ordinary, everyday, narcissistic struggles prevent us from developing the kind

CHAPTER FOURTEEN

of independence and clarity that seems to be easily available to Buffett the investor.

Narcissism is something that everybody struggles with, one way or another, throughout life. It is an attempt to make ourselves feel less insignificant by appearing to be the opposite – special and important.

The oft-painful complications of growing up in a family, going to school, finding a mate and establishing a working life can make us feel less than adequate and no more so than in our highly competitive, non-stratified modern Western world. Because we live in an open society with social mobility, our role in the world is not dictated by our caste or the jobs of our fathers or our level of aristocracy. We lack the reassuring certainty of a definite place in the scheme of things, where our definition of who we are is determined by circumstances beyond our efforts. We live in a world where self-made men are admired, where, so the myth goes, we can all make it. And further, if we don't, we have no one but ourselves to blame. On top of this, we live in an economic system that allocates resources and rewards via competition; we compete for positions in sporting teams, in schools, in universities, jobs and for partners.

I am not criticising capitalism or the way we live, but merely highlighting the reality that this world abounds with opportunities for self-doubt, comparison and disappointment. To complicate matters, we sometimes deal with our disappointments by trying to make ourselves feel less bad, which can also quickly translate into making ourselves feel more important.

The impact of this is that we become overly concerned with how we are seen by others. It weakens our independence and we become anxious about what others think of us. As this sense of discomfort builds, we increase our sense of self-importance. The result is that we need more and more to feel satisfied with ourselves. We end up hardly ever feeling that enough is enough.

The consuming nature of this reparative work leaves little space and time or interest to just be in the world. In this situation, so much of an individual's interest is used to reassure the self of its own worth. Instead of enjoying our pursuits for their own sake we entangle them with a need to reassure ourselves and others of our sense of specialness and importance. Subsequently, everything is done in the service of secondary gain (for the way in which it feeds one's ego), rather than for itself.

'For itself' is not meant to imply a totally selfless appreciation of things and people in the world. It merely emphasises that these things and people are enjoyed or treasured by virtue of the qualities that are found to be of value, rather than the way they make individuals feel important about themselves.

For an investor, this dynamic can cause him to take his eye off the ball and leave him with less than a full focus on the task at hand as well as tempt him toward investment activities that offer prestige as a focus, rather than return. It can do more than that. It can cause him to be unfaithful to his own style, to his own natural inclinations - all to be impressive or to appear to be a certain way. Buffett on the other hand, talks of keeping one's eye on the game rather than the scoreboard; and he, in his non-narcissistic way, is quite happy to simply make money at the expense of self-importance. He's as happy to make money from selling furniture as he is from owning American Express. It's not about triumph; it's about appreciating and enjoying the things that you pursue rather than using them.

The feeling of being 'less-than' can also create a reparative pressure toward perfectionism and being the best - that good enough is not enough. To be just 'ordinary' or merely who one is could be extremely painful as, clearly, that would mean being somebody who is wrong,

CHAPTER FOURTEEN

flawed or pathetic. To escape this imperative one has to be *extra* ordinary.

This is where the danger of attempting to 'heal' vulnerabilities comes in. It seems perfectly sensible and reasonable to want to heal damage and make oneself feel better about oneself. However, what happens in the narcissistic struggle is that the wound is felt so deeply that it ignites a more-than extremely energetic drive to repair. It becomes relentless and takes on a life of its own. So what could start out as a happy and legitimate attempt to repair some damage becomes a consuming project devoted to self-aggrandisement with an intensity of focus that leaves little space for the more important and subtle qualities of life.

This kind of pressure seems so absent in Buffett, who almost relishes his ordinariness. He says, 'Why search for a needle buried in a haystack when one is sitting in plain sight?'[1] It's so clever and impossibly difficult to find a needle in a haystack but he has no internal pressure pushing him toward looking especially clever. Being ordinary gives him the enormous freedom of a non-narcissistic perspective where he can just get on with the job of making money. Initially, the struggles of the individual involved in narcissistic repair are to overcome rather modest flaws. This can move on to a point where success is valued only when it is extra special. Then comes the drive to self-aggrandisement in a greedy, urgent, desperate way; a constant preoccupation with demonstrating that everything is special or perfect. It becomes difficult to put roots down properly because of a fear of missing out on something more important. The agitated, urgent, restless difficulty with compromising and staying in one place would make it impossible to spend the kind of time and energy necessary to thoroughly investigate business opportunities with the level of rigour and dedication characteristic of Buffett.

For individuals with narcissistic traits it becomes very difficult to love someone or something because the purpose of everyone and everything is to make those individuals feel more important. Typically the narcissistic person will lose interest in any person (no matter how significant that person may be) who stops making him feel important or special enough. Instead, such an individual will become riveted by the next best person or thing. The consequence is that narcissistic individuals are prevented from establishing long-term loyal connections, having a sense of place or really healing their psychic wound through mutually supportive and enriching relationships.

And so, such individuals return to the beginning because the journey of narcissism makes it impossible to form the kind of relationships that will make them feel loved for being themselves. Loving relationships can't be valued sufficiently in themselves for long enough and with enough commitment for this to occur. It is a bit like trying to fill a sieve: always leaking and always needing filling. Without the nourishment of intimate relationships that can sustain an individual, there is likely to be a more promiscuous grasping of people who must feed one's ego. This will never let one have anything approaching the working life of Buffett, who takes pleasure in the relationships he has with the people he respects and who respect him.

Buffett, without a hint of these narcissistic dynamics forms strong, ongoing, warm relationships, which he has valued and protected over a lifetime. This prevents him from flitting in and out of investments. It also allows him to form robust business associations that can endure over time, providing him with business opportunities and access to people who may enhance his enterprise. Additionally, Buffett has his own life. He is not looking elsewhere for a life. He makes compromises, lives in his own world and puts very strong roots down. He also has little fear of missing out.

A feature of narcissism that would undo Buffett, where he would lose his vital essence, would be the consequence of narcissism's

CHAPTER FOURTEEN

push toward self-importance. We see that the inside of a narcissistic individual is often a vulnerable and fragile place where there is little freedom to be oneself. If one is going to feel important, it is going to involve feeling more important than others. If the self is defined by that importance, then being more important defines the self. And, it is not only a simple matter of just being better than others, it is a matter of having to become intensely interested in the lives of others and what they have.

Someone who struggles under this burden has little chance of knowing the freedom and independence that comes from the kind of internal scorecard Buffett has. He merely gets on with his life making money and is not trying to show off or out-do anyone else. He is not preoccupied with them or their doings, which frees him to think about how he would like to do things. He can be his own man.

A central dynamic of narcissism is envy. At one level the envious aspect of narcissism is preoccupied with all that is of value being outside itself. Envy, in this sense, seems to cloud one's ability to see that one has something of value, instead only the value that lies elsewhere can be seen. On the other hand, it's also hard for the narcissist to acknowledge that there is real inherent value in another individual and he may need that individual. To acknowledge that there is inherent value in another suggests that one may lack that value; and if that's the case, one can't be the best. In this instance the narcissistic individual may attempt to cut down the value of the other person, rather than acknowledge its value, depend on it and need it.

It's therefore not difficult to see how narcissism could preclude one from depending on more competent individuals to make one rich – an essential component of the life that Buffett lives.

In an investment environment where the lure of narcissistic solutions is ever-present and hazardous, Buffett has found his way through the maze unknowingly. In a world generously endowed with narcissism, he seems to have done a pretty good job of not turning out to be a narcissist.

It may seem a bit odd to be talking about Buffett's non-narcissistic qualities when he is explicitly someone who seeks out and 'uses' (attaches himself to) other people for his own needs. Many of his relationships revolve around people with whom he has become involved in this way. One could imagine that his interest in them could diminish if they lost their capacity to make him money. Is he then not the quintessential 'user'? If he is someone who begins a lot of his important relationships in order to use them for his own needs of making himself richer, aren't we looking at a narcissist?

No.

A narcissist is someone who uses other people as a means to extend his own self-esteem. Buffett 'uses' people to make himself rich and his need to get rich seems to spare him the usual pitfalls that go with a narcissistic struggle of this kind. As discussed in Chapter One, Buffett seems to love money as a means of giving him a sense of at-homeness in the world, more for the deeper kind of soothing that it provides. It doesn't seem to be specifically ego-related.

All our relationships start from less than pure beginnings; it is what becomes of them that matters.

From the start of life we are searching to meet our needs, from the most basic to the most sophisticated. The people to whom we turn to meet these needs are most often initially seen for their capacity to meet our needs and not for their inherent value. Whether we grow to love them and value them through our ongoing instrumental contact with them, or whether the bond transcends its initial usefulness, will depend on both our own capacity for attachment and the nature of the relationship that develops. The narcissistic individual, unlike Buffett,

CHAPTER FOURTEEN

is flawed in his capacity to grow to love those he might start out using.

With narcissism, ensuring that relationships are primarily instrumental, where 'using' eclipses love and loyalty, it is unlikely that any narcissistic investor would be able to form the stable of devoted managers and co-owners that form the successful investing enterprise that is Buffett's.

The journey toward the position that Buffett so easily occupies is beautifully illustrated in the Greek mythological story of Cassius.

Cassius lived in a seemingly heavenly world, in a fertile and bountiful glade, where all his desires were constantly satisfied: food, sex, music, and beauty - he had it all. He passed his days in blissful abandon and believed himself to be the luckiest man in the universe.

After some time, he began to feel a strange restlessness, which he couldn't make sense of. He realised he was longing for a friend. He tried to distract himself but he became bored, so he ventured out of his blissful glade until he stumbled upon a woman, Miriam, rowing her boat in a stream.

He begged for her to take him with her but she explained that she lived far away in a garden she had worked very hard to create. She told him that he could come and share in her life if he promised her a baby. He agreed. But she added one last critical condition. If he were to come with her, as soon as they would reach the other side of the river where her house was, she would burn the boat and he could never return to the glade.

At this requirement Cassius froze. He pondered her request but couldn't agree.

He returned to his bountiful glade that momentarily soothed him but he lived a torturous life, before ending it...

Cassius' fatal mistake is that he can't make do. He can't accept that the life on offer from Miriam is a good enough life for him. He can't give up other opportunities for it. He has been spoilt by his fantasy life of having it all, even though it made him feel empty in the end. He could not compromise and have a real, limited woman in a real, limited life that is rich, alive and fulfilling.

All this Buffett can do with ease. He is able to be his limited self, to be at home in his own investment style and forgo all the 'innovations' and crazes of the booming investment industry. He finds 'good enough' businesses and lives with them. He commits himself to his managers. He is not frantically looking elsewhere for more in a way that detracts from his commitment to what he already has. He focuses on what he is doing for itself. And he collects more!

If there is any hope that one can invest in the way Buffett does, from a strongly independent, deeply considered place, where 'important people, and vocal people' do not have undue influence, then one has to have an exceptional freedom from the ordinary man's vulnerability to narcissistic struggles.

CONCLUSION

There's hope for us all

IF, AS THE old saying goes, the love of money is the root of all evil, then it's surprising or perhaps reassuring that we can turn to someone who has pursued money so vigorously for good advice on how to live. We have also discovered that Buffett has within him, by his very nature, the perfect combination of helpful qualities that you could ever wish to bring together in an ideal investor. He has a charismatic personality, a wonderful way with words, irresistible charm and an enormous intellect. His equal would be difficult to find.

Does this necessarily mean that all 'investment hopefuls' should pack up and go home? Or is there something to be learned from the essential features that make up Buffett's brilliance as an investor, while still remaining ourselves? Is there some way in which we can understand the nature of his exceptional ability and integrate it into our own natural style, without simply mimicking him?

In seeking an answer to these questions, I interrogated the Buffett that is revealed through his writings. I sought to discover what the essential qualities of his genius are and how they interact to create a certain kind of whole. I did this because it had always struck me as odd that so few commentators have paid any heed to his personality structure – the foundation of the man that is Warren Buffett and the source of his acclaimed actions in the world. For me, the lack of attention to these aspects reflects a widespread tendency to overlook the journey of the self – of who one really is and what one's life is really about.

CONCLUSION

It seems to me that there is great danger in rushing to take advice without placing it within the context of the individual personalities giving and receiving it. Let's take a piece of 'technical advice' to illustrate what I mean. Buffett suggests that it is important to have the capacity to survive a 50 per cent drop in price in a stock one owns. This advice works only when the person taking the advice is, like Buffett, extremely diligent and rigorous in his understanding of his stocks and the market; and not sloppy, ill-informed and prone to having a beer while watching his stocks decline by another 50 per cent, heeding the essence of Buffett's advice with ease.

If we want to be successful investors, it is not sufficient to take Buffett's advice. We need to discover who we are by questioning ourselves, looking into ourselves and finding an investing style that is respectful of who we are. This is no small challenge but is undoubtedly a worthwhile one because, if we do not understand who Buffett is and who we ourselves are, we cannot fully digest his advice.

Indeed, the avoidance of this kind of exercise could go some way to explaining why Buffett's generous advice has not helped anyone achieve close to his level of success.

If we can come to know ourselves and find a way of investing that is honest and reflective of who we really are, we have a much greater chance of succeeding. We can then feel at home there – committed, connected and engaged – to spend sufficient time developing our mastery without distractedly looking elsewhere at what the rest of the world is doing. The significance of finding a place where we belong shouldn't be underestimated. It has the capacity to hold us to our work in a powerfully connected way and also to energise us with the level of intensity that is required for major achievements.

A further surprising benefit of studying Buffett was the realisation that I was learning something more than how Buffett's qualities

CONCLUSION

facilitate the way he invests: I was learning how to live a good life. And so, in many ways, this book equally hints at what qualities promote a good life, such as loving people, being loyal, thinking independently and accepting our limits.

I have no interest in making judgements about how people should live and what should be important to each individual, and do not suggest that we should emulate Buffett, but it has struck me that there is much to be gained from the way Buffett deals with some of the biggest and most important issues in life.

Buffett's overall level of emotional maturity – his ability to accept life as it is and people as they are – is also reflected in the way he invests. And it is because he invests in this way, attuned to who he is, that he is so successful.

While I support the idea of knowing who we are and finding a way of investing that is in tune with our personalities, I am not suggesting that it is always helpful to just be the way we are. It is regrettably true that the 'way we are' is sometimes very unhelpful or destructive.

Buffett is lucky. He is lucky in the sense that he has the personality that enables him to be a good investor. He can simply 'be himself' because all the qualities he has and the way they hang together are conducive to being a great investor. Most of us are not so lucky and need to struggle to overcome those aspects of our selves that prevent us from being successful investors, whether they be our impatience, our ruthlessness or niceness. But even if it's not our natural inclination and even if we can only achieve some partial approximation in this struggle, we may give ourselves a better chance of a good life.

Of course one cannot overlook the hard work, the time and energy that Buffett has put into cultivating his gifts. But it is also true that many of us could apply ourselves with equal determination and still fall far short.

CONCLUSION

I have learned an enormous amount from Buffett and through him I have begun the lifelong journey of understanding myself. My hope is that we can all be ourselves but be real with ourselves. To acknowledge our strengths but to equally understand that some parts of who we naturally develop to be might hinder us on our path to success and contentment.

Ultimately, the qualities I have described in Buffett exist in all of us, in one way or another. Perhaps it is through our understanding of the way in which these qualities exist and interact within Buffett that we can discover how to both harness and battle these qualities in ourselves to become the kinds of investors that most naturally suit our personalities.

APPENDIX

SOME THOUGHTS ON SELLING YOUR BUSINESS[1]

This is an edited version of a letter I sent some years ago to a man who had indicated that he might want to sell his family business. I present it here because it is a message I would like to convey to other prospective sellers. W.E.B.

Dear ...

Here are a few thoughts pursuant to our conversation the other day.

Most business owners spend the better part of their lifetimes building their businesses. By experience built upon endless repetition, they sharpen their skills in merchandising, purchasing, personnel selection, etc. It's a learning process, and mistakes made in one year often contribute to competence and success in succeeding years.

In contrast, owner-managers sell their business only once – frequently in an emotionally charged atmosphere with a multitude of pressures coming from different directions. Often, much of the pressure comes from brokers whose compensation is contingent upon consummation of a sale, regardless of its consequences for both buyer and seller. The fact the decision is so important, both financially and personally, to the owner can make the process more, rather than less, prone to error. And, mistakes made in a once-in-a-lifetime sale of a business are not reversible.

Price is very important, but often is not the most critical aspect of the sale. You and your family have an extraordinary business – one of a kind in your field – and any buyer is going to recognise that. It's also a business that is going to get more valuable as the years go by. So if you decide not to sell now, you are very likely to realise more money later on. With that knowledge you can deal from strength and take the time required to select the buyer you want.

If you should decide to sell, I think Berkshire Hathaway offers some advantages that most other buyers do not. Practically all of these buyers will fall into two categories:

(1) A company located elsewhere but operating in your business or in a business somewhat akin to yours. Such a buyer – no matter what promises are made – will usually have managers who feel they know how to run your business operations and, sooner or later, will want to apply some hands on 'help'. If the acquiring company is much larger, it will often have squads of managers, recruited over the years in part by promises that they will get to run future acquisitions. They will have their own way of doing things and, even though your business record undoubtedly will be far better than theirs, human nature will at some point cause them to believe that their methods of operating are superior. You and your family probably have friends who have sold their businesses to larger companies, and I suspect that their experiences will confirm the tendency of parent companies to take over the running of their subsidiaries, particularly when the parent knows the industry, or thinks it does.

(2) A financial manoeuvrer, invariably operating with large amounts of borrowed money, who plans to resell either to the public or to another corporation as soon as the time is favourable.

APPENDIX

Frequently, this buyer's major contribution will be to change accounting methods so that earnings can be presented in the most favourable light just prior to his bailing out. I'm enclosing a recent article that describes this sort of transaction, which is becoming much more frequent because of a rising stock market and the great supply of funds available for such transactions.

If the sole motive of the present owners is to cash their chips and put the business behind them – and plenty of sellers fall in this category – either type of buyer that I've just described is satisfactory. But if the seller's business represents the creative work of a lifetime and forms an integral part of their personality and sense of being, buyers of either type have serious flaws.

Berkshire is another kind of buyer – a rather unusual one. We buy to keep, but we don't have, and don't expect to have, operating people in our parent organisation. All of the businesses we own are run autonomously to an extraordinary degree. In most cases, the managers of important businesses we have owned for many years have not been to Omaha or even met each other. When we buy a business, the sellers go on running it just as they did before the sale; we adapt to their methods rather than vice versa.

We have no one – family, recently recruited MBAs, etc. – to whom we have promised a chance to run businesses we have bought from owner-managers. And we won't have.

You know of some of our past purchases. I'm enclosing a list of everyone from whom we have ever bought a business, and I invite you to check with them as to our performance versus our promises. You should be particularly interested in checking with the few whose businesses did not do well in order to ascertain how we behaved under difficult conditions.

Any buyer will tell you that he needs you personally – and if he has any brains, he most certainly does need you. But a great many buyers, for the reasons mentioned above, don't match their subsequent actions to their earlier words. We will behave exactly as promised, both because we have so promised, and because we need to in order to achieve the best business results.

This need explains why we would want the operating members of your family to retain a 20 per cent interest in the business. We need 80 per cent to consolidate earnings for tax purposes, which is a step important to us. It is equally important to us that the family members who run the business remain as owners. Very simply, we would not want to buy unless we felt key members of present management would stay on as our partners. Contracts cannot guarantee your continued interest; we would simply rely on your word.

The areas I get involved in are capital allocation and selection and compensation of the top man. Other personnel decisions, operating strategies, etc. are his bailiwick. Some Berkshire managers talk over some of their decisions with me; some don't. It depends upon their personalities and, to an extent, upon their own personal relationship with me.

If you should decide to do business with Berkshire, we would pay in cash. Your business would not be used as collateral for any loan by Berkshire. There would be no brokers involved.

Furthermore, there would be no chance that a deal would be announced and that the buyer would then back off or start suggesting adjustments (with apologies, of course, and with an explanation that banks, lawyers, boards of directors, etc. were to be blamed). And, finally, you would know exactly with whom you are dealing. You would not have one executive negotiate

APPENDIX

the deal only to have someone else in charge a few years later, or have the president regretfully tell you that his board of directors required this change or that (or possibly required sale of your business to finance some new interest of the parent's).

It's only fair to tell you that you would be no richer after the sale than now. The ownership of your business already makes you wealthy and soundly invested. A sale would change the form of your wealth, but it wouldn't change its amount. If you sell, you would have exchanged a 100 per cent-owned valuable asset that you understand for another valuable asset – cash – that will probably be invested in small pieces (stocks) of other businesses that you understand less well. There is often a sound reason to sell but, if the transaction is a fair one, the reason is not so that the seller can become wealthier.

I will not pester you; if you have any possible interest in selling, I would appreciate your call. I would be extraordinarily proud to have Berkshire, along with the key members of your family, own...; I believe we would do very well financially; and, I believe you would have just as much fun running the business over the next twenty years as you have had during the past twenty.

Sincerely,

Warren E. Buffett

1 Berkshire Hathaway Inc Shareholder Letter, 1990.
www.berkshirehathaway.com/letters/1990.html

NOTES

CHAPTER ONE
[1] May, Simon. *Love: A history.* New Haven CT: Yale University Press, 2011.
[2] Ibid.
[3] Berkshire Hathaway Inc. Shareholder Letter, 1986.
www.berkshirehathaway.com/letters/1986.html
[4] Ibid.
[5] Berkshire Hathaway Inc. Shareholder Letter, 1984.
www.berkshirehathaway.com/letters/1984.html
[6] Nell Minow, Editor and Co-Founder of The Corporate Library, an independent corporate governance research firm, interviewed Warren Buffett for The Corporate Library's 2010 Public Funds Forum, held in Laguna Beach, California, in September 2010.
www.youtube.com/watch?v=Og12HflMdpo
[7] Ibid.
[8] Berkshire Hathaway Inc. Shareholder Letter, 1987.
www.berkshirehathaway.com/letters/1987.html
[9] Berkshire Hathaway Inc. Shareholder Letter, 1990.
www.berkshirehathaway.com/letters/1990.html
[10] Berkshire Hathaway Inc. Shareholder Letter, 1979.
www.berkshirehathaway.com/letters/1979.html
[11] Berkshire Hathaway Inc. Shareholder Letter, 1978.
www.berkshirehathaway.com/letters/1978.html
[12] Berkshire Hathaway Inc. Shareholder Letter, 1986.
www.berkshirehathaway.com/letters/1986.html
[13] Buffett Partnership Letter, 1963.

CHAPTER TWO
[1] Berkshire Hathaway Inc. Shareholder Letter, 1983.
www.berkshirehathaway.com/letters/1983.html
[2] Berkshire Hathaway Inc. Shareholder Letter, 1987.
www.berkshirehathaway.com/letters/1987.html
[3] Berkshire Hathaway Inc. Shareholder Letter, 1992.
www.berkshirehathaway.com/letters/1992.html
[4] Berkshire Hathaway Inc. Shareholder Letter, 1988.
www.berkshirehathaway.com/letters/1988.html

CHAPTER THREE
[1] Heidegger, Martin. *Being and Time*, trans. by Joan Stambaugh, revised by Dennis J Schmidt. Albany: State University of New York Press, 2010.
[2] Husserl, Edmund. *Phenomenological psychology.* Boston: Martinus Nijhoff, 1977. (First edition published 1925.)
[3] Berkshire Hathaway Inc. Shareholder Letter, 1987.
www.berkshirehathaway.com/letters/1987.html

NOTES

[4] Buffett, Warren. Partnership Letter, 1964.

CHAPTER FOUR
[1] Berkshire Hathaway Inc. Shareholder Letter, 1990. www.berkshirehathaway.com/letters/1990.html

[2] Hazlitt, Henry. *Economics in one lesson.* New York: Three Rivers Press, 1988.

CHAPTER FIVE
[1] Foroohar, Rana. 'Warren Buffett Is on a Radical Track,' *Time*, Monday, Jan. 23, 2012. www.time.com/time/magazine/article/0,9171,2104309-6,00.html (accessed 17 June 2012).

[2] Berkshire Hathaway Inc. Shareholder Letter, 1978. www.berkshirehathaway.com/letters/1978.html

[3] Berkshire Hathaway Inc. Shareholder Letter, 1984. www.berkshirehathaway.com/letters/1984.html

[4] Berkshire Hathaway Inc. Shareholder Letter, 1986. www.berkshirehathaway.com/letters/1986.html

[5] Berkshire Hathaway Inc. Shareholder Letter, 1993. www.berkshirehathaway.com/letters/1993.html

[6] Berkshire Hathaway Inc. Shareholder Letter, 1985. www.berkshirehathaway.com/letters/1985.html

[7] Berkshire Hathaway Inc. Shareholder Letter, 1988. www.berkshirehathaway.com/letters/1988.html

CHAPTER SIX
[1] March, James G and Diane L Coutu 'Ideas in art. A conversation' *Harvard Business Review*, 1 October 2006.

[2] Berkshire Hathaway Inc. Shareholder Letter, 1989. www.berkshirehathaway.com/letters/1989.html

[3] Buffett Partnership Ltd Letter, 1966.

[4] Berkshire Hathaway Inc. Shareholder Letter, 2000. www.berkshirehathaway.com/2000ar/2000ar.pdf

[5] Berkshire Hathaway Inc. Shareholder Letter, 1986. www.berkshirehathaway.com/letters/1986.html

[6] Berkshire Hathaway Inc. Shareholder Letter, 1984. www.berkshirehathaway.com/letters/1984.html

[7] Berkshire Hathaway Inc. Shareholder Letter, 1981. www.berkshirehathaway.com/letters/1981.html

CHAPTER SEVEN
[1] Berkshire Hathaway Inc. Shareholder Letter, 1996. www.berkshirehathaway.com/letters/1996.html

[2] Gladwell, Malcolm. *Outliers.* New York City: Little, Brown and Company, 2008.

[3] Berkshire Hathaway Inc. Shareholder Letter, 1999.

NOTES

www.berkshirehathaway.com/letters/1999htm.html

[4] Warren Buffett, Second Annual Letter to Limited Partners: The General Stock Market Picture in 1957.

[5] Berkshire Hathaway Inc. Shareholder Letter, 1991. www.berkshirehathaway.com/letters/1991.html

[6] Ibid.

[7] Berkshire Hathaway Inc. Shareholder Letter, 1989. www.berkshirehathaway.com/letters/1989.html

[8] Berkshire Hathaway Inc. Shareholder Letter, 1987. www.berkshirehathaway.com/letters/1987.html

CHAPTER EIGHT

[1] Warren Buffett, Second Annual Letter to Limited Partners: The General Stock Market Picture in 1957.

[2] Berkshire Hathaway Inc. Shareholder Letter, 1984. www.berkshirehathaway.com/letters/1984.html

[3] Berkshire Hathaway Inc. Shareholder Letter, 1996. www.berkshirehathaway.com/letters/1996.html

[4] Ibid.

[5] Berkshire Hathaway Inc. Shareholder Letter, 1986. www.berkshirehathaway.com/letters/1986.html

[6] Berkshire Hathaway Inc. Shareholder Letter, 1998. www.berkshirehathaway.com/letters/1998htm.html

[7] Berkshire Hathaway Inc. Shareholder Letter, 1983. www.berkshirehathaway.com/letters/1983.html

[8] Berkshire Hathaway Inc. Shareholder Letter, 1996. www.berkshirehathaway.com/letters/1996.html

[9] Berkshire Hathaway Inc. Shareholder Letter, 1987. www.berkshirehathaway.com/letters/1987.html

[10] Berkshire Hathaway Inc. Shareholder Letter, 1985. www.berkshirehathaway.com/letters/1985.html

[11] Berkshire Hathaway Inc. Shareholder Letter, 1983. www.berkshirehathaway.com/letters/1983.html

CHAPTER NINE

[1] Berkshire Hathaway Inc. Shareholder Letter, 1987. www.berkshirehathaway.com/letters/1987.html

[2] Berkshire Hathaway Inc. Shareholder Letter, 2006. www.berkshirehathaway.com/2006ar/2006ar.pdf

[3] Berkshire Hathaway Inc. Shareholder Letter, 1989. www.berkshirehathaway.com/letters/1989.html

[4] Berkshire Hathaway Inc. Shareholder Letter, 1977. www.berkshirehathaway.com/letters/1977.html

NOTES

CHAPTER TEN
[1] Berkshire Hathaway Inc. Shareholder Letter, 2006. www.berkshirehathaway.com/2006ar/2006ar.pdf

[2] Griffin, James. 'Is frugality a virtue?' *Unesco Courier*, vol 51, issue 1, January 1998, p 10.

CHAPTER ELEVEN
[1] Berkshire Hathaway Inc. Shareholder Letter, 1985. www.berkshirehathaway.com/letters/1985.html

[2] Berkshire Hathaway Inc. Shareholder Letter, 2000. www.berkshirehathaway.com/2000ar/2000ar.pdf

[3] Berkshire Hathaway Inc. Shareholder Letter, 1986. www.berkshirehathaway.com/letters/1986.html

CHAPTER TWELVE
[1] Berkshire Hathaway Inc. Shareholder Letter, 2012. www.berkshirehathaway.com/2012ar/2012ar.pdf

[2] Neuhauser, Richard. *The early history of greed: The sin of avarice in early Medieval thought and literature*. New York: Cambridge University Press, 2000.

[3] Ibid.

[4] Baba, Meher. *Discourses*. North Myrtle Beach, CA: Sheriar Press, Inc, 1987.

[5] Boris, Harold. *Envy*. Lanham: Jason Aronson, 1994.

CHAPTER THIRTEEN
[1] Boris, Harold. *Envy*. Lanham: Jason Aronson, 1994.

[2] Titelman, Peter. 'A phenomenological comparison between envy and jealousy' *Journal of Phenomenological Psychology*, 1981.

[3] Berkshire Hathaway Inc. Shareholder Letter, 2006. www.berkshirehathaway.com/2006ar/2006ar.pdf

[4] Coffin, Harold. *Coffin's Needle*. New York: The Associated Press, 1970.

CHAPTER FOURTEEN
[1] Berkshire Hathaway Inc. Shareholder Letter, 1993. www.berkshirehathaway.com/letters/1993.html

Acknowledgements

THESE ARE MORE than just acknowledgements; these are my most sincere thanks, with the deepest sense of appreciation and love for you all.

First, to Peter Parker, for your guidance, for mentoring me and for everything else. None of this would have happened without you. You have given me a foundation for my life. Eternal thanks are not enough.

To my dad, Bori, for giving me the freedom and space to explore all my loves, however unconventional; for your gentle way and also for your quiet and patient support and love.

To my beautiful wife, Amina, the love of my life since I was eleven years old. From the beginning you filled my world with unexpected life and vibrancy. You made me feel whole and valuable, and that I mattered. You still do. Thank you for loving and supporting me, and for creating such a beautiful family for us.

To my mum, Helen, for all your warmth, generosity and so much love and goodness. You have given me a 'home' in the world. No words could ever capture what you mean to me or what you have given to me. Everything that I am is because of you.

To Madeline Lass for all your wonderful help, insight and encouragement.

To Keri, Vaughan, Sarah and Helen at Hardie Grant, for helping to bring everything together.

To Richard Davies for starting me off on this profound journey.

And to so many other people who enrich my life in so many ways.

Thank you,
Nic

Published in 2014 by Hardie Grant Books

Hardie Grant Books (Australia)
Ground Floor, Building 1, 658 Church Street
Richmond, Victoria, 3121
www.hardiegrant.com.au

Hardie Grant Books (UK)
Dudley House, North Suite
34-35 Southampton Street
London WC2E 7HF
www.hardiegrant.co.uk

All rights reserved. No part of this publication may be reproduced, stored in a retrieval system or transmitted in any form by any means, electronic, mechanical, photocopying, recording or otherwise, without the prior written permission of the publishers and copyright holders.

The moral rights of the author have been asserted.

Copyright © Nic Liberman
Copyright illustrations © Craig McGill

National Library of Australia Cataloguing-in-Publication entry
Liberman, Nic
Being Warren Buffett: Life Lessons from a Cheerful Billionaire / Nic Liberman
ISBN 9781742708904
Buffett, Warren–Capitalists and financiers–Investments–Life skills–Success
332.6

Cover and text design by Vaughan Mossop
Typesetting by Hayley Coghlan
Typset in Leitura News 9.5/15 pt
Printed in China by C & C Offset Printing

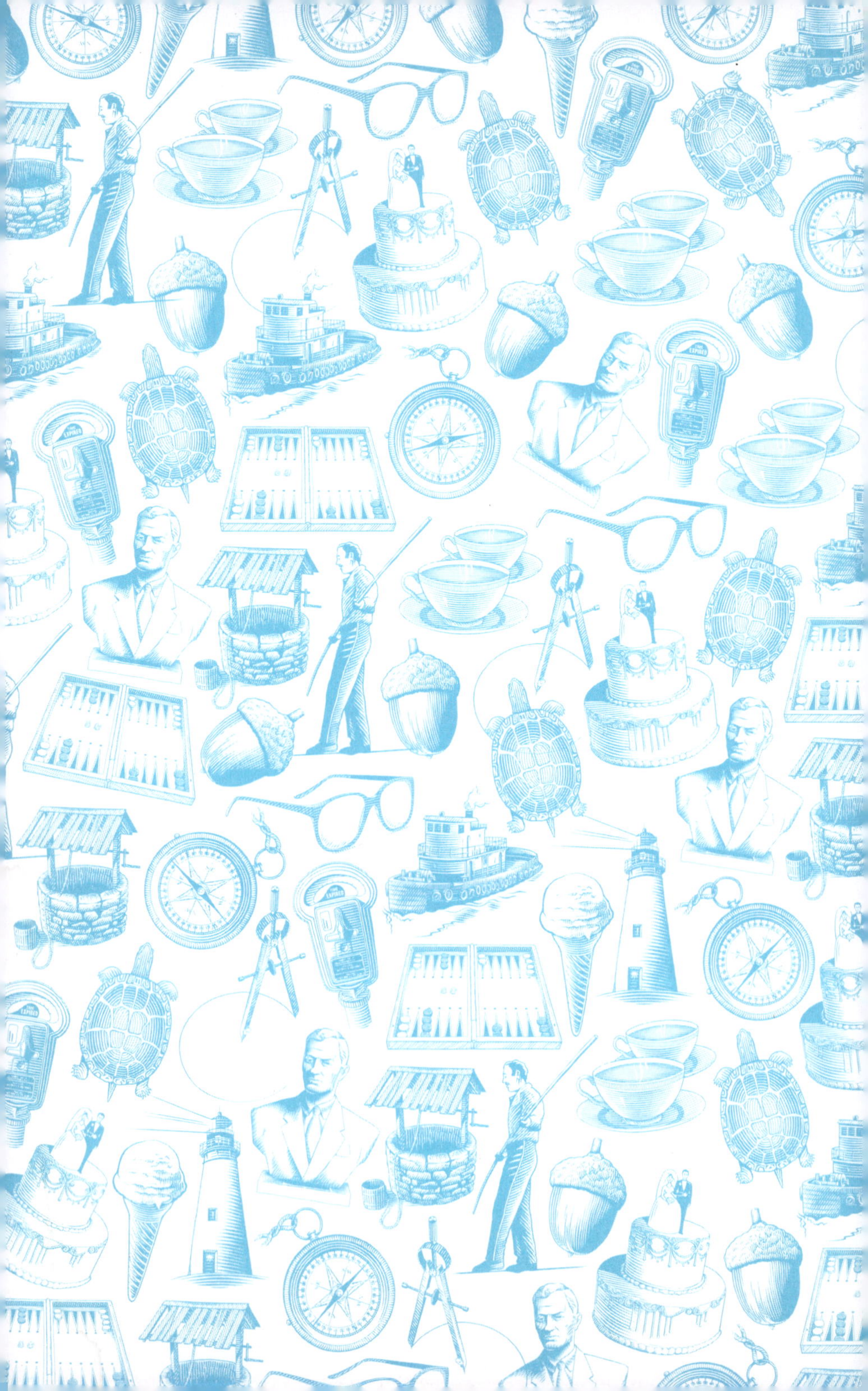